Workbook 7

Improving Your Organization's Success

Manage Activities
Diploma
S/NVQ Level 5

Institute of Management Open Learning Programme

Series editor: Gareth Lewis
Author: Bob Johnson

the Institute
of Management

FOUNDATION

Pergamon
Open
Learning

Pergamon Open Learning
An imprint of Butterworth-Heinemann
Linacre House, Jordan Hill, Oxford OX2 8DP
A division of Reed Educational and Professional Publishing Ltd

℞ A member of the Reed Elsevier plc group

OXFORD BOSTON JOHANNESBURG
MELBOURNE NEW DELHI SINGAPORE

First published 1997

British Library Cataloguing in Publication Data
A catalogue record for this book is available from the British Library

ISBN 0 7506 3666 1

Typeset by Avocet Typeset, Brill, Aylesbury, Bucks
Printed and bound in Great Britain

Contents

Series overview

The Institute of Management Open Learning Programme is a series of workbooks prepared by the Institute of Management and Pergamon Open Learning for managers seeking to develop themselves.

Comprising seventeen open learning workbooks, the programme covers the best of modern management theory and practice, and each workbook provides a range of frameworks and techniques to improve your effectiveness as a manager, thus helping you acquire the knowledge and skill to make you fully competent in your role.

Each workbook is written by an experienced management writer and covers an important management topic or theme. The activities both reinforce learning and help to relate the generic ideas to your individual work context. While coverage of each topic is fully comprehensive, additional reading suggestions and reference sources are given for those who wish to study to a greater depth.

Designed to be practical, stimulating and challenging, the aim of the workbooks is to improve performance at work by benefiting you and your organization. This practical focus is at the heart of the competence based approach that has been adopted by the programme.

The structure of the programme

The design and overall structure of the programme has two main organizing principles, both of which are closely linked to the national standards for management developed by the MCI (Management Charter Initiative).

First, the workbooks are grouped according to the key roles of management.

- Underpinning the management standards are a series of **personal competences** which describe the personal skills required by all managers, which are essential to skill in all the main functional or key role areas.
- **Manage Activities** describes the principles of managing processes and activities, with service to the customer as an essential part of this.
- **Manage Resources** describes the acquisition, control and monitoring of financial and other resources.
- **Manage People** looks at the key skills involved in leadership, developing one's staff and managing their performance.

- **Manage Information** discusses the acquisition, storage and use of information for communication, problem solving and decision making.

In addition, there are three specialized key roles: **Manage Quality, Manage Projects** and **Manage Energy**. The workbooks cover the first two of these. Unlike the four primary key roles above, these are not compulsory for certificate, diploma or S/NVQ requirements, but provide options for the latter.

Together, these key roles provide a comprehensive description of the fundamental principles of management as it applies in any organization – commercial, maintained sector or not-for-profit.

Second, the programme is organized according to **levels of management**, seniority and responsibility.

Level 4 represents first line management. In accredited programmes this is equivalent to S/NVQ Level 4, Certificate in Management or CMS. Level 5 is equivalent to middle/senior management and is accredited at S/NVQ Level 5, Diploma in Management or DMS. There are two S/NVQs at Level 5: Operational Management and Strategic Management. The operations role is focussed internally within an organization on the maintenance of systems and standards of output, whilst the strategic role is focussed on the whole organization, including the external operating environment, and looks at setting directions.

Together, the workbooks cover all the background knowledge you need to have for all units of competence in the MCI standards at Level 4 and Level 5 (apart from the specialized units in the key role Manage Energy). They also provide skills development and opportunities for portfolio building.

For a comprehensive list of workbooks, see page ix. For a comprehensive list of links with the standards, see the *User Guide*.

How to use the programme

The programme is deliberately designed to be flexible and can be used in a variety of ways:

- to update on important management topics and themes, or develop individual skills: as the workbooks are grouped according to themes, it should be easy for you to pick out one that suits your needs

- as part of generic management development programmes: you can choose the modules that fit the themes of the programme

■   **as part of, and in support of, accredited competence-based programmes.**

For N/SVQs at both Levels 4 and 5, there are options in the combinations of units that make up the various awards. By using the map provided in the *User Guide*, individuals will be able to select the workbooks appropriate to their specific needs, and their chosen accreditation options. Some of the activities will help you provide evidence for your portfolio; where we think this is the case, we give the relevant reference to the standards.

For Certificate or CMS, Diploma or DMS, individuals should choose modules that not only meet their individual needs but also satisfy the requirements of the delivering body and the awarding body.

You may need help and guidance in these choices, and the *User Guide* sets out the options and advice in much more detail. A fuller description of the potential uses of this material in evidence gathering and portfolio building can also be found in the *User Guide*, as can a detailed description of the contents of each workbook.

Workbooks in the Institute of Management Open Learning Programme

Personal Competences (Levels 4 and 5)

  1 *The Influential Manager**
  2 *Managing Yourself**

Manage Activities (Level 4)

  3 *Understanding Business Process Management*
  4 *Customer Focus*

Manage Activities (Level 5)

  5 *Getting TQM to Work*
  6 *Leading from the Front*
  7 *Improving Your Organization's Success*

Manage Resources (Level 4)

  8 *Project Management*
  9 *Budgeting and Financial Control*

Manage Resources (Level 5)

  10 *Effective Financial and Resource Management*

Manage People (Level 4)

  1 *The Influential Manager*
  2 *Managing Yourself*
  11 *Getting the Right People to do the Right Job*
  12 *Developing Yourself and Your Staff*
  13 *Building a High Performance Team*

An asterisk indicates that a particular workbook also contains material suitable for a particular key role or personal competence over and above that where it is principally designated.

Links to qualifications

S/NVQ programmes

This workbook can help candidates to achieve credit and develop skills in the key role of managing activities at level 5, and covers the following units and elements:

A8 Evaluate and improve organizational performance
A8.1 Develop measures and criteria to evaluate your organization's performance
A8.2 Evaluate your organization's performance
A8.3 Explain the causes of success and failure in organizational strategies

Certificate and Diploma programmes

This workbook, together with the other level 5 workbooks on managing activities (5 – *Getting TQM to Work* and 6 – *Leading From the Front*), covers all of the knowledge required in the key role Manage Activities for Diploma and DMS programmes.

Links to other workbooks

Other workbooks in the key role Manage Activities at Level 5 are:

5 *Getting TQM to Work*
6 *Leading From the Front*

and at Level 4:

3 *Understanding Business Process Management*
4 *Customer Focus*

Introduction

Continuous improvement – challenge or temptation?

The title of this workbook is seductively attractive. Except in organizations where motivation and commitment are at rock-bottom, most people want the business to succeed. So, if success is a shared goal, improved success must be even more desirable.

Ironically, though, the quest for improvement – and particularly continuous improvement – is often the principal cause of lost motivation and reduced commitment. As we point out in Section 1 of this workbook, improvement involves change. Most people are suspicious of change and find it threatening. Change is expected to generate winners and losers. Most people would like to be among the winners but are afraid that they will find themselves among the losers.

Consequently, this workbook follows these key themes. The first relates to an objective evaluation of the need for improvement. Then in Section 2, we offer a series of checklists of performance achievement. But we also suggest that these numbers by themselves are not enough. They need to be compared, either with in-house historical data to identify trends and patterns, or, better, with industry standards through the medium of benchmarking, to identify whether improvement is really necessary.

Our second theme is the need for performance improvement to be seen in the light of long-term strategic objectives. Obvious though this may sound in theory, the practical difficulties involved are significant. There are several reasons for this:

- **The impact of external change** in Section 4 of this workbook, we examine the contribution of environmental analysis to the strategic planning process. The environmental factors we explore relate to politics, economics, social trends, technological developments and competitor activity. None of these is controllable, all have the potential to have a major impact and none can be predicted with total accuracy. Consequently, as we explore in Section 5 of the workbook, there is a limit to the objective, analytical approach to strategic planning and any emphasis, which for some may be quite worrying, on hunch and instinct. This means of course, that long-term organizational direction can only be exposed in broad terms – perfectly satisfactory for long-range planning but not so helpful to the specification of short-term performance measures.

■ **Improvement requires action**   by extension, short-term improvement requires short-term action. However, as we point out in Section 3, failure to achieve short-term performance targets can easily result from strategic rather than operational weaknesses. Thus, while we stress in several places the importance of remedial action being taken as low down the organization as possible, it is often the case that such action involves more than a 'quick fix'. The remedy requires major surgery, not just a sticking plaster.

■ **Improvement as a discontinuous process**   in a strategic context, the future may require radical changes in direction. This is one of the topics of Section 5, although we are careful to distinguish between the destructive 'I'm bored. Let's change something' approach to management and the more considered one that takes action when it is clear that the current strategic direction is no longer relevant. However, performance improvement as a continuous process assumes a linear progression. And this is not always the case.

Our final theme is implicit in the first two themes. It is the human dimension of performance improvement and appears in several sections of this workbook.

In Section 1 we stress the need for change and improvement to be seen as justified by those who will be involved. We also point out that staff involved in the improvement process must have the skills to implement change effectively.

In Section 5, we examine a range of corporate-level activities that will have an impact on the extent to which people in the organization understand where it is heading, are committed to and able to contribute to improvement.

In Section 6, we examine the whole subject of organizational culture. We explore the different factors that affect culture and their suitability to different kinds of organizational activity and environment. We also review the steps and risks involved in bringing about a shift in organizational culture.

Finally, in Section 7, we look in some detail at a central cultural question: that of organizational ethics and values. We suggest that an organization's values will determine the sort of people who work there, what decisions are taken, how they are taken and for whose benefit. We stress that there is no such thing as 'absolute' values, and that whether actions and decisions are right depends on their consistency with the values that the organization has adopted and promoted.

Objectives

By the end of this workbook, you should be able to:

- identify in broad terms the style of control mechanisms relevant to your organization
- recognize, develop and introduce suitable performance indicators to monitor critical areas of functional performance
- introduce relevant and effective methods of performance improvement
- recognize the variety of potential factors contributing to performance shortfalls
- differentiate between operational factors susceptible to short-term remedies and strategic factors requiring long-term attention
- apply a strategic problem-solving model
- evaluate your organization's environment
- assess the speed of change in that environment
- evaluate the relevance to your environment of some current philosophies of change
- identify the need for and take relevant strategic decisions related to choice and development of markets, supplier relations and staff management
- recognize the nature of your organization's culture
- identify the sources of that culture
- critically evaluate its current suitability
- recognize the actions needed to change culture
- identify the ethical school(s) to which your organization's values belong
- evaluate their consistency
- assess the match between published values and how they are modelled
- describe those ways of addressing the issue of culture in a multinational organization

Section 1   If it ain't bust, don't fix it

Where are we now? Where should we be?

Two fundamental and opposing principles underlie the process of monitoring performance. The first principle asserts that the objective of performance monitoring is to identify the organization's success in achieving its goals, objectives and targets. The implications of this principle are that current objectives and targets will result in the achievement of long-term goals and that, therefore, performance in line with current objectives and targets is adequate for the organization's survival and success.

The second principle is that the organization's success depends on continued improvements in customer focus, quality, productivity, cost reduction and profitability. Consequently, the way forward depends on continued updating of objectives and targets, to ensure that progress is consistent with changes in the marketplace, improvements in competitive offerings and overall developments in the external world.

ACTIVITY 1

Which approach does your organization take to performance monitoring:

management by objective? OR

external adaptation?

Is that approach suitable to your industry and environment?

FEEDBACK

Of course, there are no right answers to these questions. However, in a rapidly changing environment, they do have major implications for the frequency with which objectives and targets are updated. At the same time, it would be unacceptable and impractical to be updating objectives continually. Even where organizations do their updating on a three-monthly or half-yearly basis, line managers still complain that 'Head Office is moving the goal posts again'.

This leaves us in a predicament when it comes to setting objectives and targets. The conundrum is how to set objectives that are consistent with a changing environment. Predictably, Tom Peters (1987) resolves the issue by moving away from quantitative measures that reflect the status quo to measures that quantify responsiveness to the environment. His prescription for monitoring performance advocates:

1 Assign each business unit and department the task of developing in thirty days five rough, unconventional paper-and-pencil measures of what's going to be important to their unit's ability to support the firm's mission.
2 Use the measures, in rough form, in formal reviews. Insist that two-thirds of the new measures emphasize (a) customers (e.g. quality, service, listening), (b) flexibility/responsiveness; (c) innovativeness and (d) the relative increase/decrease in the value of the workforce's skills, taken as a whole.

Peters' suggestions for unconventional measures to monitor performance are shown in Table 1.

Table 1 Performance measures

Description	Measure
Niche creation	Number of 'differentiators' added to each product every ninety days.
Quality	Relative perceived product quality; poor-quality cost; rewards based on quality goal. Devise quality measures in every unit. Evaluate suppliers on the basis of quality.
Service	The ten attributes of customer satisfaction (frequency of surveys, format of surveys, content, design of content, involvement, comprehensiveness, combination, relation to reward, publication of results, individual contribution); customer evaluation of the intangibles; the lifetime value of a customer.
Responsiveness	Speed of response to customer needs; percentage of customers covered by tight (electronic or other) linkages; new links (electronic or other) added to each product every ninety days.

Description	Measure
Listening	Informal listening ('call three customers every week').
Factory as marketing area	Customer visits to factory; factory manager and non-manager visits to customers.
Sales, service and distribution	Time spent with sales and service people; rate at which additions are made to sales and service force; number of franchises/distribution presumed.
Small starts	Number of small starts; percentage of time/R&D budget devoted to small starts.
Pilots	Number of pilot tests of anything going on in each area.
Competitive analysis	Number of ideas 'swiped' from competitors per month.
Word of mouth	Percentage of ad/marketing budget devoted to word of mouth.
Support innovators	Number of awards to innovators; number/percentage of awards to unsung supporters of innovators per month.
Support past failures	Number of awards for interesting failures; constructive defiance of rules.
Share of revenue from new products	Percentage of revenue coming from new products introduced in the last twelve, twenty-four, twenty-six months.
Teams	Percentage of people in team configurations.
Recognition	Number of recognition acts/events per month.
Training	Hours/money devoted to skill upgrading.
Compensation	Percentage of total compensation from profit-distribution bonus plan; pay for knowledge programme.
Middle management role	Number of acts of boundary-bashing; number of awards going to boundary-bashers.
De-bureaucratize	Number of demeaning and debilitating regulations removed per month; number of amenities added to each facility per month; your 'housekeeping' scored vis-à-vis competitors.
Manage by example	Time spent per day/week on top priority.
Visible management	Percentage of time out of the office; percentage of time with customers/front-line people.
Line focus	Number of line versus number of staff at meetings; line versus staff salaries; time spent with line people.
'What have you changed'	Amount of things changed; formally evaluate everyone accordingly.

You may find these suggestions too radical for immediate adoption! Nevertheless, they do provide a valuable challenge to the more traditional performance measures we shall be considering later in this section.

The next scene-setting factor we need to consider is the relationship between short-term and long-term performance. In Workbook 7 of this series, we pointed out that planning time-scales are reducing in length and that, whereas historically short-term plans were for three years and long-term plans for ten years, current preferences are typically for twelve and thirty-six months. However, this does not change the fact that it is still essential for short-term performance to contribute to the achievement of long-term strategic objectives. So, for example, Rover's success in achieving its sales targets in the mid-1990s did not prevent its take-over by BMW.

This presents us with three challenges. The first is the need to monitor short-term performance against quantified objectives. The second is the need to monitor long-term performance against both quantitative and qualitative goals and objectives. And the third is to achieve consistency between the two. Or, in other words, ensuring that short-term efficiency is really good enough to achieve long-term effectiveness and survival.

'Creative dissatisfaction': good or bad?

Tom Peters' proposals for alternative performance measures, and our emphasis on the need for consistency between short-term and long-term objectives may have prompted you to question the relevance, both of your current operations and of your performance monitoring systems. Of course, both of these questions are crucially relevant.

ACTIVITY 2

How confident are you that your organization's current operations will achieve its long-term goals?

To what extent do your short-term performance measures monitor the right things?

To what extent do your long-term performance measures monitor the right things?

Nevertheless, when all of the current management literature is emphasizing discontinuous change and the need to adapt successfully to it, it is tempting to assume that whatever we are doing now is not good enough and to find some alternatives.

And yet ... Before making internal changes, it is essential to stop for long enough to ask why and whether they are truly necessary. Internal changes may result from:

- environmental change
- scope for increased productivity, greater efficiency or cost reduction
- or low boredom threshold or a bright but unnecessary idea on the part of management

The last cause may be justified, at least superficially, by reference to one of the other two. However, such justification is bound to be seen through and resented by those responsible for carrying out the resultant change. As Derek Pugh (1986) points out:

Effective reasons for changes are those that can be accepted by many of the interest groups and people who will be involved. For example, needs which can be demonstrated to flow from changes in the firm's environment (changes in customers' behaviour, competitors' tactics, Government policies) will find greater acceptability as being relevant to all, than purely internally generated changes which are more likely to be viewed in the political system (i.e. how it will affect the power, status, prestige of the group).

Consequently, the process of 'creative dissatisfaction' – continually looking for new and better ways to achieve results that are already being achieved – is a mixed blessing. Vincent Nolan (1987), a consistent advocate of change, acknowledges this:

Because change is exciting, there is a temptation to change things that are already working well, often without any net benefits. This usually happens when the problem-solving process has been misdirected – directed not at the area of need, but at the area in which it is easiest to find new solutions.

A good safeguard is to make a balanced appraisal of the existing situation before starting on problem solving. The balanced appraisal will identify all the good features of the present situation, as well as the areas that need improvement. Problem solving can then be directed at those areas, with the explicit understanding that any new solution must retain the strengths of the present situation, or offer such outstanding benefits that their loss is more than offset.

One of the key strengths of an existing and successful performance monitoring system is, of course, the commitment and support of those who operate it. So, as Derek Pugh points out, a main factor when considering change is its impact on people:

Will the change alter job content?

Will it introduce new and unknown tasks?

Will it disrupt established methods of working?

Will it rearrange group relationships?

Will it reduce autonomy or authority?

Will it be perceived to lower status?

Will it be established without full explanation and discussion?

ACTIVITY 3

What changes have recently been introduced in your organization?

Were the results better or worse than before?

Was there an overriding reason for them?

Were people informed and consulted?

Was the change really necessary?

How could the change process have been improved?

'Do nothing' as a valid decision

So far, we have been discussing the desirability or otherwise of changes to the performance monitoring system. However, the points we have made:

- the need to have a valid reason for change
- the requirement for those involved to support change
- the importance of balancing the gains and losses of change

apply equally to changes in operational tactics and longer term strategy.

Assuming a monitoring system that works (and we will explore what that entails a little later), there are three possible outcomes from comparing performance with targets:

- performance exceeds target
- performance meets target
- performance fails to meet target

In the first two cases, the obvious response is to celebrate and wait for the next set of results. This may be the right response, but not necessarily. Before assuming that no action is necessary, it is important to check:

- whether a performance that exceeds target places unacceptable strain on the organization's resources
- whether a performance that exceeds target is indicating too low a target, or else the start of a trend
- whether on-target performance indicates too low a target, or is an exception to the overall pattern
- whether the achievement of short-term targets is sufficient to achieve the organization's long-term goals and objectives

Where performance has failed to meet target, there are again some important questions to ask:

- is this failure an exception to a trend?
- what is the extent of the deviation and is it significant?
- does the deviation stem from an optimistic target, a phasing issue, or an environmental change?
- is this area of performance central to the achievement of the organization's long-term goals and objectives?

Armed with this information about the patterns and significance of deviations and the reasons for them, it is possible to make some decisions about corrective action. Such action may involve:

- revising the targets
- initiating further investigation into long-term trends
- changing work methods and practices to improve performance
- allocating additional resources
- postponing action until more data is available, or the deliberate decision that no action is necessary

This last possibility is sufficiently important to warrant further comment. The first four points all involve taking action. By definition, such action will be disruptive and time-consuming. It will need to be planned, communicated, implemented, monitored and controlled. It is therefore only justified if the cost of not taking action exceeds that of the action itself. While those costs are difficult to quantify, they are necessary to have in order to ensure that corrective action in a given situation is worth while.

If yours is a formal, hierarchical organization, you may find it more difficult to initiate corrective action than to prevent it. Nevertheless, the more autonomy your people have, and the more committed they are to achieving success for their part of the organization, the more likely it is that they will spend so much time and effort on action to correct minor deviations that they do not have enough to spare for the day-to-day running of the business.

ACTIVITY 4

At what level do people in your organization have responsibility for initiating corrective action?

Do they tend to:

❑ ignore the need for action?
❑ over-react to deviations?

How closely are short-term performance measures linked to the long-term goals of the organization?

How confident are you that current short-term performance will achieve the organization's long-term goals?

If you are not confident. What is at fault:

❑ the long-term goals?

❑ the short-term targets?

❑ the short-term performance?

Goals, targets and objectives in times of change

Goldsmith and Clutterbuck (1958) summarize their findings from research into the UK's most successful companies as follows:

The tension between control and independence is inevitable. What our most successful companies seem to have done is use that tension constructively to create a feeling of maximum autonomy while keeping tight rein on the areas that matter for their market and type of organisation. All freedom is relative; it brings with it responsibilities which of themselves become restraints. Creating the right framework of control and independence is one of the ingredients that helps these companies to extract extraordinary performance from very ordinary people.

While comparing Plessey with AGB, the authors identify two contrasting extremes of approach to planning and control:

One (Plessey) relies on the detailed but relatively flexible five-year plan to set visible targets and define routes to achieve them. It achieves its goals by following the plan as far as possible and revising its route (and sometimes the objectives too) at least every year, and usually on a continuous basis. Growth is primarily organic and internal, rather than by acquisition..

The other can best be described as an opportunistic approach, which sets broad-brush objectives, commits everyone to achieving them, and seizes any chance to move towards them. This approach relies heavily on the availability of cash resources, generated by operations that are already successful. Unit managers are constantly evaluating new projects, from which further growth may come, instead of concerning themselves deeply about the operational problems of their unit as it is. Their growth focus tends to be more external, through buying in talented people who have new ideas and financing their efforts, or through direct acquisition of smaller companies with the potential to expand.

A number of themes, however, are common to both approaches:

- a limited number of key corporate objectives, widely communicated and understood
- few controls exercised by the centre, but with the requirement that line managers should adhere strictly to them
- close attention to the adoption of controls that are specific and relevant to the long-term success of the business. Control of capital expenditure appears consistently. High-tech companies (for example STC and Racal) emphasize technological innovation, while Sainsbury strictly controls hygiene
- a tight and obvious link between the achievement of targets and personal reward
- the perception by managers that the control system frees them to concentrate on the things that matter

Goldsmith and Clutterbuck identify four factors that underpin an effective control system:

- tight controls on finance, to ensure that the money goes where it will be most effective in generating more
- constant feedback of results
- close attention to business planning
- setting high standards and expecting people to stick to them

So how does all this relate to change? In five ways.

1 setting only a few corporate objectives, but ensuring that they are understood, provides line managers with the freedom and information to respond positively and creatively to change

2 just a few central controls, mainly financial, ensure focus on survival and growth

3 business-specific controls gain commitment through their relevance, but also avoid managers wasting time on activities not linked to rapid adaptation

4 results that are fed back not only constantly but also quickly allow early identification and treatment of problems

5 the current environment demands high standards if organizations are to succeed

ACTIVITY 5   A8.1

How many corporate objectives does your organization communicate?

How well are they understood?

Do they provide suitable actions and decisions from the line?

How many controls are exercised by the centre?

What is their main focus?

Are they all necessary?

Do controls measure factors that are specific and important to the organization?

Is the achievement of targets rewarded?

Does this happen in a way that encourages the repetition of successful behaviour?

Do managers see the control system as:

❑ restrictive?

❑ supportive?

How quickly are results fed back?

Is this quickly enough?

How do you organization's standards compare with competitors?

Summary

In this section we have considered the rationale for monitoring performance in organizations. Specifically, we have covered:

- two rationales for monitoring performance – success in delivering goals, and continuous adaptation
- short-term versus long-term planning
- pressures for change
- requirements for different levels of control systems
  goals, targets and objectives

Section 2 Evaluating short-term performance

Breaking down the organization

The management standards to which we are working do not, strictly speaking, refer to short-term performance measures. It might even be argued, based on some of the content of the previous section, that the design and monitoring of such measures should be left to the line. Nevertheless, references elsewhere in the standards to delegation, guidance and monitoring suggest the need to touch on the subject, if only briefly. In this section, therefore, we shall have a brief look at some of the key performance indicators from which your organization might want to select in order to monitor short-term performance in the constituent functions of the organization – finance, marketing, operations and personnel. We stress the need to select carefully. We will recall our earlier points that performance measures need to be specific to the organization and that relevant indicators are those which measure contribution to the overall achievement of the organization's strategic goals.

Financial controls

Complete Activity 6 which asks you which of the following financial controls are particularly relevant to your organization.

ACTIVITY 6

Checklist of financial controls

Tick those controls that are relevant to your organization. Also tick those which, though relevant, are not currently in place.

	Tick if relevant	Tick if not in place
Return on capital	❏	❏
Overall gross profit	❏	❏
Overall net profit	❏	❏
Cost of goods sold	❏	❏
Capital expenditure	❏	❏
Revenue expenditure	❏	❏
Gross turnover	❏	❏
Labour costs	❏	❏

We have limited the controls in Activity 6 to those which are either purely financial, or which reflect the overall performance of the business. More detailed controls related to individual cost or profit centres now follow.

Marketing controls

Activity 7 provides a checklist of the marketing controls used to monitor short-term performance indicators in your organization.

ACTIVITY 7

Checklist of marketing controls

Tick those controls that are relevant to your organization. Also tick those which, though relevant, are not currently in place.

	Tick if relevant	Tick if not in place
Sales force		
Gross revenue per member	❏	❏
Profit per member	❏	❏
Weekly calls	❏	❏
Travel time v. contact time v. desk time	❏	❏
Product and market knowledge	❏	❏
Sales interview skills	❏	❏
Presentation and demonstration skills	❏	❏
Planning skills	❏	❏

	Tick if relevant	Tick if not in place
Orders by member	❏	❏
Order size	❏	❏
Sales per call	❏	❏
Profit per call	❏	❏
Advertising and promotion		
Cost of advertising	❏	❏
Cost of promotion	❏	❏
Advertising recall	❏	❏
Advertising comprehension	❏	❏
Impact on buying predisposition	❏	❏
Impact on brand switching	❏	❏
Impact on corporate image	❏	❏
Distribution		
Cost of physical distribution	❏	❏
Profitability per channel	❏	❏
Product development		
Development cost per new product	❏	❏
Time from launch to profitability	❏	❏
Proportion of new product failures	❏	❏
Cost per launch	❏	❏
Percentage of total revenue from new products	❏	❏
Percentage of total profit from new products	❏	❏
Speed of introduction	❏	❏
Marketing research		
Cost of research	❏	❏
Accuracy of information	❏	❏
Speed of information	❏	❏
Relevance of information	❏	❏
Sales forecasting		
Short-term reliability	❏	❏
Medium-term reliability	❏	❏
Long-term reliability	❏	❏
Pricing		
Gross profit per product	❏	❏
Net profit per product	❏	❏
Comparison with competitors	❏	❏

	Tick if relevant	Tick if not in place
Customer satisfaction		
Level of satisfaction	❑	❑
Number of complaints	❑	❑
Customers gained	❑	❑
Customers lost	❑	❑

Operational controls

Operations is a general term to describe the production function. Depending on the activity of the organization, it may refer to:

- manufacturing
- retailing
- warehousing and distribution
- source provision
- patient care
- education services
- administration

The following checklist is an attempt to summarize some, but certainly not all, of the possible operational controls across a range of these sectors.

ACTIVITY 8

Checklist of operational controls

Tick those controls that are relevant to your organization. Also tick those which, though relevant, are not currently in place.

	Tick if relevant	Tick if not in place
Overall costs of production	❑	❑
Productivity by employment category	❑	❑
Level of materials wastage	❑	❑
Cost of inventory	❑	❑
Equipment downtime	❑	❑
Spare utilization	❑	❑
Purchasing costs	❑	❑
Capacity usage	❑	❑
Proportion of bought-in components	❑	❑
Age of stock/stockturn	❑	❑

	Tick if relevant	Tick if not in place
Speed of throughput	❑	❑
Achievement rate	❑	❑
Waiting time	❑	❑
Length of stay	❑	❑
Proportion of patients cured	❑	❑
Numbers of qualifications gained	❑	❑
Error level	❑	❑
Volume of throughput	❑	❑
Speed of response	❑	❑

Personnel controls

Activity 9 provides some key performance indicators related to the personnel function of your organization.

ACTIVITY 9

Checklist of personnel controls

	Tick if relevant	Tick if not in place
Staff motivation		
Labour turnover	❑	❑
Volume of official grievances	❑	❑
Arrange time with organization	❑	❑
Vacancies unfilled	❑	❑
Absentee levels	❑	❑
Incidence of strikes/industrial unrest	❑	❑
Staff development		
Availability of training	❑	❑
Take-up of training	❑	❑
Level of internal promotion	❑	❑
Volume of on-job training	❑	❑
Quality of induction	❑	❑
Satisfaction with training	❑	❑
Manpower planning	❑	❑
Arrange age by category	❑	❑
Numbers of suitable candidates for key positions	❑	❑
Success of internal promotions	❑	❑

	Tick if relevant	Tick if not in place
Length of time from promotion to resignation	❏	❏
Reward structure		
Balance between salary and benefits	❏	❏
Balance between salary and incentives	❏	❏
Competitiveness of salaries	❏	❏
Wage/salary differentials	❏	❏
Safety		
Number of accidents	❏	❏
Health and safety infringements	❏	❏
Frequency of checks	❏	❏
Availability of training	❏	❏

Conclusions

The checklists we have offered go some way towards offering a system to monitor the overall and functional performance of an organization. The factors we have suggested reflect a fairly traditional and well-researched system of controls. Of course, there may be others that are equally or more relevant to your organization. Nevertheless we would make two points:

- performance monitoring is a waste of time if it does not result in remedial action to address shortfalls or problems identified by the process
- the responsibility for performance monitoring at this level rests with functional or line staff. Depending on the structure, culture and hierarchy of your organization, this may mean managers or individual staff members. The purpose of this review has been simply to enable you to take a proactive view of what is happening lower down the organization.

Summary

In examining short-term performance, we have developed a series of indicators of performance as checklists in a number of areas:

- finance controls
- operational controls
- personnel controls

Section 3 From short term to long term

Remedial action – nature and purpose

As we have just pointed out, a performance monitoring system has no value if it does not result in remedial action. But what sort of action? And what should it be intended to achieve?

The performance controls we proposed in the last section are effective indicators of variances from a norm, target or ideal. Or, at least, they should be, provided that the organization has some kind of historical, strategic, industry or general benchmark against which to compare performance. What they do not do, however, is identify either why the variance has occurred – or what needs to be done to correct the variance.

ACTIVITY 10

	Target	Actual
Machine output per hour	230	210

What possible reasons can you think of which might explain this nine per cent shortfall against target?

FEEDBACK

We hope your list was a long one! Possible explanations are:

- the failure or extended downtime of one or more machines
- unscheduled service or repairs
- lack of required spares inventory
- lower than forecast demand
- operator strike or work to rule
- lack of operators
- inexperienced or untrained operators
- unrealistically high output targets
- targets take no account of scheduled maintenance

As you will have noticed, this single performance measure – hourly machine output against target – identifies that there is a problem, but does not go far in helping to pin down either its nature or its causes.

To do this will take you into a formal process of problem solving and decision making. You may be familiar with the model shown in Figure 1.

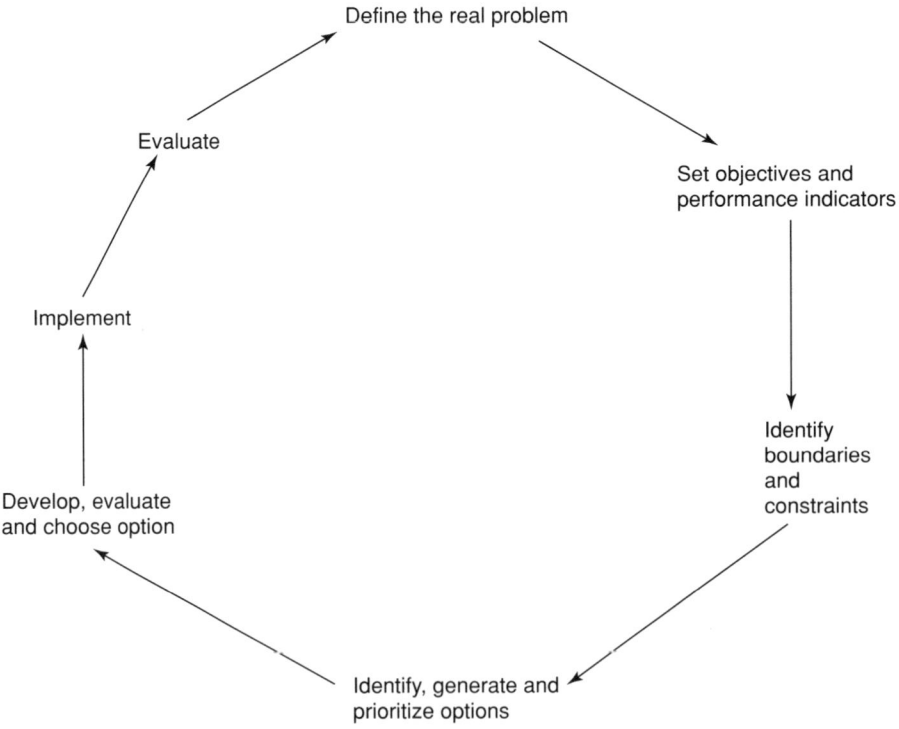

Figure 1   A model for problem solving

The stages of the model are summarized below.

- **Define the real problem**   Failure to achieve the production target is a symptom rather than a problem. Defining the real problem involves digging beneath the symptoms to isolate their causes.
- **Set objectives and performance indicators**   What do you want to change? How do you want things to be in the future? These are the objectives for a solution. The possible causes of the production shortfall imply there may be a range of problems, demanding several solutions, each with a number of objectives. Performance indicators will be the measures you will use to see if you have achieved your objectives.
- **Identify boundaries and constraints**   How far-reaching is the problem? Which parts of the organization does it affect? What constraints, if any, limit your choice of solutions (for example, time, cost, resource availability, expertise, legal constraints)?
- **Identify, generate and prioritize options**   Options are the possible ways of solving the problem. It is worth while generating as long a list as you can, before selecting those which are worth taking further.
- **Develop, evaluate and choose option**   Take the potentially valuable solutions a step further. Consider their impact and implications. Then choose the options that provide the best fit in meeting your objectives.
- **Implement**   Having made your choice take the necessary action to resolve your problems.
- **Evaluate**   Monitor the progress of the solution, making further changes if necessary. Has it met your objectives? What lessons can you draw for the future?

This problem-solving model (often called the 'Dutch' model, though for no apparent reason) can be used successfully by people at any level in an organization. However, at a junior level, its emphasis on taking a holistic view – identifying and treating underlying causes, the way it encourages users to think broadly about the impact and implications of a problem – tends to raise difficulties. The objection is often that the scale of the problem and the options that might represent truly effective solutions are outside the authority of junior staff.

The apparently simple production shortfall example shown in Activity 10 highlights this difficulty. Potentially, the causes are cross-functional and the solutions strategic as well as operational.

However, dealing with performance variances from target is a more complex issue than might at first appear. For most organizations, the strategic plan looks something like a house of cards – with lower-level plans supporting the next level up, as well as those on either side. Consequently, failure to achieve a single target has the potential to bring the whole structure down.

CASE STUDY

The following is an example from WH Smith's Retail Group strategy. In the 1980s, the company defined itself, not as a self-service store, but as one that offered 'assisted self-selection', with an emphasis on customer advice and service. However, such a definition depends, self-evidently, on the availability of knowledgeable staff. The company allowed the differential between city-centre and provincial pay rates to erode. As a result, it became increasingly difficult to fill vacancies in city-centre stores, particularly in London. Thus, managers in these stores were often unable to achieve one of their key performance measures, which was the presence of a shop-floor team in line with the establishment.

ACTIVITY 11

What operational and strategic impacts would you expect from this failure to achieve targeted staffing levels?

Operational

Strategic

FEEDBACK

At an operational level, the level of shop-floor staff impacted on a store's ability to achieve its sales turnover targets. Induction training for new staff who did join was either skimped or ignored, from the need simply to have even untrained staff on the floor. Stock-control procedures were often poorly applied.

At a strategic level, the overall image of the company suffered, as did its ability to sell more complex products, with implications for both product range and profitability. Because city-centre stores bring in the most business, overall turnover fell. And the company started to lose its ability to deliver 'assisted self-selection', which was one of its main marketing differentiators.

Consequently, even a simple performance variance from a single indicator may require, not only short-term operational action to deal with the immediate symptom, but also longer term strategic action to address the underlying causes and wider effects.

Identifying causes

This is the point at which we set out to define the real problem by identifying the causes underlying the symptoms shown up by the performance monitoring system. It is worth remembering a consistent message throughout the literature on performance monitoring and management information systems which is that what they do is ask questions. They do not provide the answers.

Let us return to the production variance illustrated in Activity 10; we asked you to brainstorm the possible causes. Activity 12 expands this exercise.

ACTIVITY 12

What action could you now take to confirm or reject the possible causes you identified?

FEEDBACK

The short answer is to access some alternative sources of data or information. Some of it will be immediately available — everyone will know if there is industrial unrest in the factory, for example. Other data will come from elsewhere in the performance monitoring system. Some may not.

Activity 13 lists the other possible causes we suggested for the production shortfall. What other data would you access to confirm or deny their contribution to this symptom?

ACTIVITY 13

Possible cause	Other data to check
Failure of one or more machines	
Extended downtime of one or more machines	
Unscheduled service or repairs	
Lack of spares	
Lower than forecast demand	
Lack of operators	
Inexperienced or untrained operators	
Unrealistically high targets	
Targets ignore schedule maintenance	

FEEDBACK

Most production monitoring systems will include details of which machines, and how many, are in action at particular times. Some may include details of time spent under service or repair – both planned and remedial. If the system does not include this information, it may be necessary to do some more research – in other words, ask the right questions of the right people! This may also highlight any shortage of spares, although that issue might also prompt some further questions about inventory management and reference to the inventory control system.

Lower than forecast demand will be shown-up by sales performance data, although once again this raises some bigger questions about marketing strategy. If sales are down:

- is the product out-of-date?
- are competitors promoting heavily?
- are prices currently uncompetitive?
- is the advertising not doing the job?
- has a major account gone elsewhere?
- if so, why?
- has something affected salesforce performance?

A lack of operators, or too many who are inexperienced or untrained, will emerge from some of the personnel indicators we listed in Activity 9.

Answers to our questions about the realism of the output targets and whether these take account of scheduled maintenance can best be gained by looking at the process by which the production function has constructed its operational plan.

What we have done here, as a result of examining thoroughly an apparently simple failure to achieve target, is to embark on a comprehensive performance audit.

Of course, not all variances will require such a detailed examination. Nevertheless, as a senior manager responsible for the long-term success of your organization, you should be aware of:

- the quality and value of the data available to your people for monitoring short-term performance
- how they interpret and apply that data
- the limits of authority within which individuals at different levels are able to solve problems
- the extent to which short-term solutions within their authority may be influenced by strategic questions
- the extent to which those questions are recognized and addressed and the level at which that happens, if it does happen

Many turn-round initiatives in a range of sectors from national government to healthcare to manufacturing have identified through a process of workforce consultation that a major source of both under-performance and employee frustration is management's failure to recognize and address the underlying causes of shop-floor problems. Not only that, but they have also highlighted the fact that often the workforce thinks it knows the answers 'but we don't have the authority and management won't listen to us'.

The workforce's answers may or may not be suitable or practical. Nevertheless, current trends in organizations towards delegation of responsibility and control and a 'bottom-up' approach to planning and decision making chime well with the self-evident truth that the person operating a piece of equipment is better placed to identify quickly what is wrong with it – and, quite probably, why and how it can be fixed – than a supervisor or technician without the same detailed experience. Equally, operators who cannot meet their production tallies 'because production planning keep changing the lines on my machine' may be simply revealing management's failure to communicate how the business works – or may be highlighting a fundamental problem in the process.

ACTIVITY 14   A8.2

How effectively does your performance monitoring system highlight issues of concern?

How easy is it to separate symptoms from problems?

How much attention does management pay to recognizing and addressing strategic questions raised by operational variances?

To what extent are junior staff involved in defining and solving problems?

How satisfied are you with that level of involvement?

Setting objectives, identifying constraints

We have put these two stages of the problem-solving model together because, while it is tempting to treat them separately, there is in fact a close link between them.

That link is best explained by contrasting two distinct schools of thought on problem solving. The first, which emphasizes an analytical approach, is exemplified by C.H. Kepner and B.B. Tregoe in their book *The Rational Manager* (McGraw-Hill, 1965). Kepner and Tregoe define a problem as 'a deviation from the norm'. This has been our starting point for the use of performance measures because, by definition, performance variances are deviations from the norm. Analytical problem solving emphasizes the use of quantitative measures to identify the nature, resulting cost and seriousness of a problem and to evaluate potential solutions. Kepner and Tregoe's definition encourages a tight focus on a specific problem and seeks to eliminate surrounding considerations.

The creative approach to problem solving defines a problem as 'the difference between where we are and where we want to be' (Nolan, 1987). It emphasizes creative and lateral thinking and the mind-set we described earlier as 'creative dis-satisfaction'. It has been, implicitly, the theme of the earlier part of this section.

Analytical problem solving sets objectives by describing the way things would be if the deviation from the norm were eliminated. It acknowledges and acts within given limitations – of time, resources and budget, for example.

Creative problem solving encourages us to disregard limitations and to think the unthinkable. Two factors promote a preference for creative problem solving in the context of this workbook. The first is the point, developed at length in Workbook 6 of this series, that significant and discontinuous changes are taking place in organizational life and the wider environment. These changes go a long way towards discrediting the idea of 'a norm' and suggest instead that the way forward is not to restore the status quo, but to seek innovative and better ways of doing things.

The second factor is the fact that, even in the most hierarchical and traditional organization, the higher up the management ladder we progress, the more the job involves managing uncertainty. Decisions become more complex, their impact more long term and the likelihood of their success more difficult to quantify. At the same time, flatter structures and the removal of layers of management, coupled with quickening environmental change, are forcing more junior members of staff increasingly to confront similar levels of uncertainty.

Of course, in the real world, practical problem solving involves both analytical and creative approaches. Problem definition involves an element of analysis. Generating solutions requires creativity. Selecting the best is again analytical. However, the process we have been advocating – of recognizing the broader and longer term implications of problems and acknowledging that sometimes operational problems require strategic solutions – overlays the analytical control of both problem definition and solution selection with a creative element.

This creative bias influences both objective and constraints. If the objective for a solution is not 'how can we put this right?' but rather: 'how can we bring about more general improvement?', the way the objective is specified obviously changes significantly.

In the same way, the allocation of resources available to solve a 'little local difficulty' will be much smaller than if the solution is a strategic one that brings major benefits elsewhere.

Nevertheless, whether you or your staff are dealing with a problem that is genuinely no more than a deviation from the norm, or whether you are seeking a broader strategic improvement, the solution objectives still need to be:

- specific
- measurable
- time-based

They also need to be timely! The drawback of the broad view we have been advocating is that it offers the temptation to postpone solving the problem until a bigger initiative deals with it. If the problem is losing you money, reducing customer satisfaction or demotivating staff, you may need to take quick and dirty action until the big improvement is in place. In that case, you will be setting and working to two sets of objectives, one for the immediate response and the other for the strategic initiative.

Similar considerations apply to constraints. It may be necessary to be strict in limiting the resources available for implementing a temporary response, on the basis that this will be overtaken by the longer term solution.

Lack of sufficient attention to objectives, resources and constraints has led organizations down two opposing and equally destructive, problem-solving routes. The first is to be so intimidated by the enormity of the problem that the organization fails to set comprehensive objectives for the solution and ends up committing huge resources to implementing a solution that ultimately fails at enormous cost. It might be argued that the failure of the infamous 'poll tax', implemented by the Conservative government under Mrs Thatcher, comes into this category. Not only did the policy fail to address the key objective that the tax should be easy and efficient to collect, it also ignored the constraint of public opinion, which led to its abandonment.

The alternative, and perhaps more common, error can be described as the sub-optimization of solutions. This involves allowing the solution adopted to be determined by the constraints rather than by the objectives to be achieved. An extreme example of this is the development of rotary engines for motorcycles. Their major advantage was their elimination of the vibration caused by traditional engine design – an important benefit. However, those manufacturers that incorporated rotary engines seriously under-estimated the technical complexity they required, in the race to get them on the market. As a result, the designs guzzled fuel and broke frequently. They were withdrawn.

ACTIVITY 15   A8.3

Does your organization typically see problems as 'deviations from the norm' or 'differences between the way things are and the way we want them to be'?

How consistent is this view with the degree of change facing your organization?

Does the view of problems vary at different levels of the organization?

How consistent is that with the extent of delegated authority?

Are problems typically solved quickly enough?

What examples are there in your organization's history of initiatives failing because objectives were not considered carefully enough?

How could that have been avoided?

What examples are there of sub-optimization of solutions?

How could that have been avoided?

Summary

In the transition from thinking about short-term objectives to long-term objectives, we have outlined the importance of remedial action, and responsibility for performance monitoring. Generally, where there is a deviation from expected performance, remedial action is indicated. We have:

- set out a problem-solving model
- identified two approaches to solving problems – analytical and creative
- highlighted the relative importance of constraints and objectives

Section 4   Predicting long-term performance

Will 'good enough' now be 'good enough' in the future?

In Workbook 6 of this series, we emphasized the move in the organizational environment from gradual, predictable change to rapid, discontinuous change. Two references from Tom Peters (1987) will illustrate the point:

In 1987 and for the foreseeable future, there is no such thing as a 'solid' or even substantial lead over one's competitors. Too much is changing for anyone to be complacent. Moreover, the 'champ to chump' cycles are growing ever shorter – a 'commanding' advantage, such as Digital Equipment's current edge in networks that allows vast numbers of computers to interact with one another, is probably good for about eighteen months at best.

There are two ways to respond to the end of the era of sustainable excellence. One is frenzy: buy and sell businesses in the brave hope of staying out in front of the growth industry curve ...

The second strategy is paradoxical – meeting uncertainty by emphasizing a new set of basics: world-class quality and service, enhanced responsiveness through greatly increased flexibility, and continuous short-cycle innovation and improvement aimed at creating new markets for both new and apparently mature products and services.

Nothing is predictable ... The prices of the major currencies, once stable within 1% over decades, now swing 5% a week and 50% a year. The prices of energy, agricultural products and metals are also volatile.

So we don't know from day to day the price of energy or money. We don't know whether protection or default will close borders making a mess of global sourcing and trade alike or whether global financing will open things up further. We don't know who our competitors will be, or where they will come from.....

Technology is yet another wild card affecting every aspect of doing business. As mentioned, it has revolutionized financing. It has also forever changed:

1   Manufacturing ...

2   Design ...

3   Distribution ...

4   Product definition ...

*On the consuming end of things, more uncertainty is added. Tastes are changing:
(1) thanks to the Japanese, Germans and others, there is a vastly increased
awareness of quality; (2) the rapid rise in the number of women in the workforce and
of two wage-earner families leads to new needs (e.g. convenience goods and services);
(3) changes in the kinds of jobs available and, hence in the distribution of incomes,
may create something like a two-class society with an increased number of 'haves'
demanding greater variety and quality, and an increased number of 'have-nots'
demanding more durable basic goods, in the face of increasingly poor prospects and
(4) with a TV or two in every home, and a car or two in most driveways, the demand
for these products is shifting from a desire for the product per se, almost regardless of
quality, to a demand for customized alternatives with special features tailored for ever
narrower market segments.*

Peters is always both stimulating and challenging. But it is important to take
account of a few issues:

- he is generalizing from American experience
- he was writing ten years ago
- he is discussing a trading rather than a not-for-profit environment
- his examples are deliberately chosen to provoke

Use the next activity to evaluate the relevance to your organization of Peters'
assertions.

ACTIVITY 16

To what extent would you consider the environment Peters is describing as
typical of that in which your organization operates?

How far does the situation of 1987 as Peters describes it reflect that of the
late 1990s?

If yours is a trading organization, to what extent is it facing the challenges of unpredictable access to markets, difficulty in foreseeing the nature and source of competition, uncertainty and speed of change in consumer tasks?

If yours is a not-for-profit organization, how far is it facing volatility in energy prices and funding availability? Is technology changing the nature of the services you provide? Are you needing to respond to changes in the workforce and the emergency in society he describes of 'have' and 'have not' classes?

Do you think Peters is exaggerating?

FEEDBACK

Most of those questions were specific to your organization. So it is not possible to provide any general comments on your responses. However, it is possible to make some broader points about the speed and nature of environmental change.

- In the UK, planning time-frames generally are reducing in length, in recognition of the perception that long-term change is now too difficult to predict accurately.
- The impact of individual environmental changes is both quicker and shorter. For example, many organizations in the early 1990s were gearing-up to cope with falling numbers of young people expected to enter the workforce, a trend caused by an ageing population and a decline in birth rate. In fact, this undoubted demographic change was overtaken by rising unemployment caused by changes in the economic environment.
- The emphasis in the UK on introducing greater competition into sectors such as local government, nationalized industries, health and education has necessitated major and discontinuous change in these sectors.
- UK authors such as Charles Handy (*The Age of Unreason, The Future of Work*) are stressing the speed and discontinuity of change in the UK environment and the need for revolutionary rather than evolutionary responses to it on the part of organizations.

Consequently, while it might be right to accuse Peters of exaggeration – after all, he has points to make and books to sell! – it would be dangerous to discard his assertions as irrelevant to current UK reality.

In Workbook 6 of this series, we presented an exhaustive analysis of the different environmental factors likely to need organizational responses. We suggested that, whether yours is an international, national or local operation, it would be subject to the following pressures and influences:

- **Political**   Political actions and decisions may open or close markets, make them less or more attractive. If you are part of a not-for-profit organization, they may change your tax situation or influence the demand for your services. If historically yours has been a government operation or nationalized industry, political decisions may change your status.

- **Economic**   The level of economic success, whether international, national, or local, will influence customer spending power, the advisability of expansion, the nature of demand, the availability of funding, the reward structure necessary to attract staff.

- **Social**   Social changes may increase or decrease your customer base, change your customer profile and their requirements from you, affect staff availability, influence your physical distribution network.

- **Technological**   Technology may change the nature of your products and services, the demand for them, the way they are produced and delivered, their cost and value.

- **Legal**   Legislation may impact on what your organization is allowed or not allowed to do. New legislation may change working practices, priorities or customer or employee perceptions of what is to be expected, accepted or condoned.

- **Environmental**   Interpreted as 'care for the physical environment', environmental influences affect a range of organizational considerations from the choice of raw materials, to manufacturing methods, to choices of physical distribution channels, to the format of packaging and energy usage.

To this range of external factors we can add the nature and activity of competitors and, as Tom Peters stresses, customer requirements and expectations as a portmanteau category.

The analysis we have just offered raises three fundamental questions:

- how much attention does your organization pay to monitoring environmental factors?
- how effectively does it respond to changes in those factors?
- how sensitive are managers and staff in the organization to environmental change and the need to respond appropriately to it?

Try answering that question now in Activity 17.

ACTIVITY 17

How much attention does your organization pay to monitoring environmental factors?

How effectively does it respond to changes in those factors?

How sensitive are managers and staff to environmental change?

How appropriately do they respond to it?

Analysing the nature of the external environment and the changes taking place within it is an essential precursor to identifying the opportunities and threats that it presents to the organization. A wide range of sources of information are available to support such an analysis.

Information about political trends – international, national and local – is readily available, in the form of opinion polls, publications such as Hansard for national politics, records of local government meetings and decisions, the stated policies and objectives of different parties and media coverage, both factual reporting and editorial comment.

Economic data is equally easy to obtain – from national sources such as the UK's *Employment Gazette* or the Central Stationery Office's *Monthly Digest of Statistics*, to international sources such as the IMF's *International Financial Statistics*, to local government data, information from local Chambers of Commerce and national trade associations. The information may deal with broad topics such as:

- rates of inflation
- price movements for raw materials, energy or commodities
- movements in retail prices
- unemployment levels
- wage rates

Or with more specific subjects such as the demand for individual products or services.

Social data include the demographic composition of the population as a whole and of the workforce, educational achievement, the factors influencing buying decisions and the way people spend their time. These data are readily available from, for example, the census and market research polls.

Access to technological information requires regular study of technical studies and reports and attendance at conferences.

Important legal judgements are reported in the quality newspapers and in the *Law Report*. New legislation can be tracked through Hansard.

Social attitudes to the physical environment are frequently the subject of media coverage and opinion polls, while trends in markets and competition are covered by professional and trade associations and market research companies.

Knowing what is happening in the external environment is, however, only the first step in taking organizational decisions. The second is to translate this awareness of what is happening in the wider world into the opportunities and threats that it presents to the organization. This step takes us from analysis to judgement by recognising the interplay of different environmental factors and deciding their impact on the organization.

The following case studies provide two examples, one commercial and one drawn from the not-for-profit sector.

CASE STUDY

IBM, until the 1980s was the supplier of choice for mainframe computers and had made the decision to continue to concentrate on this segment of the IT market. However, it overlooked the increasing speed and computing power of personal computers, brought about by major improvements in the technology. They also under-rated user frustration with reliance on a central computing function – a social factor, if you like. From a marketing viewpoint, they failed to recognize the fact that new companies such as Apple had achieved a high reputation for the user friendliness and capacity of their personal computers. As a result of all those misjudgements, IBM became close to losing its presence in the business computing market.

CASE STUDY

The Church of England is our not-for-profit example. Church attendance has been dropping for a long time, with a consequent fall in revenue from collections. At the same time, the number of retired clergy is increasing, resulting in the growth of money needed for pensions. The Church Commissioners therefore decided to reinvest some of the Church's funds, moving them from safe, but low-return investments into commercial rented property. Unfortunately, this decision was taken just before the crash in demand for city-centre offices. As a result, instead of being able to fund clergy pensions from revenue, the Church was forced to fund them by selling-off some of its property, at a time when the market was seriously depressed.

Of course, the news from environmental analysis is not always bad. Economic, social or political change may open up new market opportunities. Demographic change may improve the availability of suitably qualified staff. Competitors may withdraw from the market.

ACTIVITY 18

How might your organization improve its understanding of the environment?

What sources of relevant data are available other than those currently used?

How effectively does your organization analyse environmental factors to identify opportunities and threats?

How might that process be improved?

Let us now return to the question with which we started this section. The answer to 'will good enough now be good enough in future?' depends on a range of considerations. If you accept the assertion of Tom Peters and others that environmental change is breathtakingly fast, far-reaching and fundamentally unpredictable, then the answer is either 'no' because current responses will be inadequate for the future environment; or else the question is irrelevant, because current activities will have no place in a radically different environment.

The answer is also 'no' if, like many other organizations nowadays, yours is following a process of continuous improvement with emphasis on quality codes and, perhaps, ISO 9000.

On the other hand, you may believe that your organization is operating in a far more stable environment than the change givers are suggesting. In that case, at least some current activities and processes may remain perfectly good enough for the foreseeable future.

Even if your organization is facing significant environmental change, turning it on its head may well be counter-productive. One major government department in the UK faced with cuts in funding, a reduced international role and the loss of traditional civil service job security, has, over the last fifteen years, introduced a bewildering range of initiatives:

- outsourcing
- competitive tendering
- downsizing
- delayering
- closure of several establishments
- a redefinition of its mission and goals
- major cultural change
- new approaches to performance assessment, training and development

The results have been extensive demotivation, the expensive failure of several projects that were introduced with inadequate thought and a general lack of direction. While there was an undoubted need to respond to environmental change, those responses have in reality, seriously reduced the department's effectiveness.

ACTIVITY 19

What examples can you think of in your organization or elsewhere, of ill-considered responses to change?

What were the results?

Having examined the environmental analysis that makes up half of an organization's analysis of its situation, we will now move on to the second half – the internal appraisal.

Quality and excellence – truth or fiction?

You may well have recognized the process we have been following as a SWOT analysis. Having identified the *opportunities* and *threats* facing the organization, derived from the environment in which it operates, the next stage is to evaluate its internal resources to assess the *strengths* and *weaknesses* they present.

An internal appraisal of strengths and weaknesses should involve an objective and critical analysis of such aspects of the organization as:

■ management
■ labour
■ products and services
■ production or delivery methods
■ distribution
■ finance
■ physical assets and resources

- systems
- plans
- research and development
- capital structure

Michael Armstrong (1990) also adds the following items:

- cost structure
- market share
- customer loyalty
- organization
- employee relations
- flexibility
- quality
- customer service

Each of these aspects should be examined in detail. So, for example, an examination of management would include an assessment of experience, levels of skill and training, age and the effectiveness or otherwise of the organization's succession planning. An examination of physical assets and resources would include an assessment of suitability, age, cost of replacement and the flexibility to adapt to new products or systems.

It is important to recognize that conclusions drawn from an internal appraisal should be relative not absolute. In other words, all aspects of the internal operation – methods, systems and resources – should be assessed by comparison with three further factors

- relevance and suitability to the achievement of the organization's objectives
- match with the demands of the environment, in particular the opportunities and threats offered
- the quality and standards of other similar or competing organizations

---

ACTIVITY 20   A8.1

What processes does your organization use to carry out its internal appraisal?

What comparisons does it use?

How satisfied are you with the approach?

Why?

How might it be improved?

It is this issue of relativity that raises doubts about many of the current buzz-words in the management literature – two of which we included in our title for this unit. A selection of quotes will clarify the point.

Winning companies innovate continuously. Among our survey participants, 84% characterise themselves as frequent innovators. In addition, the survey respondents report that, on average, more than a quarter of their sales are from products that didn't exist five years ago; of these 40% did not exist a decade ago. They said further that, on average, their companies account for 40% to 60% of all the major innovations in their industries. (Clifford and Cavanagh, 1985)

Some organisations fear the future; others embrace it with enthusiasm. Although our sample of top companies clearly all have a distinct and stable culture to carry around with them, they also tend to enjoy experimentation within the areas they understand. They have a general openness to new ideas, although not always to ideas from outside; they value innovations that advance the corporate mission. They tend to see innovation not as another overhead that the company needs to stay in business, but as a flexible tool in the competitive game. (Goldsmith and Clutterbuck, 1985)

In the re-invented corporation, quality will be paramount. (Naisbitt, 1985)

In observing the excellent companies and specifically the way they interact with customers, what we found most striking was the consistent presence of obsession. This characteristically occurred as a seemingly unjustifiable over-commitment to some form of quality, reliability or service. (Peters and Waterman, 1982)

To these often-repeated terms – innovation, excellence, quality, service – we can add customer focus, added value, continuous improvement.

So how do we use them as benchmarks against which to measure the strengths and weaknesses of the organization?

Historically, the marketing literature has pointed out that, for example, price-cutting, increased advertising expenditure and customer promotions are expensive and only lead to short-term competitive advantage. Long-term advantage, on the other hand, results from close attention to customer requirements and enhanced product and service benefits.

However, in a world where innovation, excellence, quality, service, customer focus, added value and continuous improvement have become either the norms or the targets for organizations, the argument for them based on competitive advantage ceases to apply. In addition, there is a growing recognition that these attributes cost money.

The debate then becomes complicated. Since internal strengths and weaknesses are relative and need to be assessed by comparison with the environment and standards elsewhere, it is obvious that organizational superiority will be lost as other organizations catch up and overtake. Re-establishing superiority, or at least priority will then require further investment.

Two conflicting views now apply to the quality and excellence issue. The first is that continuous improvement is so firmly embedded in many organizational cultures that customers expect it. But they will need to recognize that they are also paying for it.

The second is that customers' expectations of quality and excellence are finite and that they fully recognize the costs involved. By extrusion, therefore, customers are happy to accept lower standards, provided these are made explicit and bring benefits in the form of lower prices.

ACTIVITY 21

What is your organization's attitude to these issues of innovation, quality, excellence, etc.?

What has been the impact on customer satisfaction?

Is that attitude sustainable?

Is it affordable?

Summary

In this section we have moved on to a consideration of the prediction of long-term performance. Specifically, we have covered:

- the impact of uncertainty on long-term planning
- monitoring external environment for opportunities and threats
- evaluation of the strengths and weaknesses of internal methods, systems and resources
- setting criteria for internal resources
- the importance of quality and excellence

Section 5 Priorities for long-term improvement

Strategic, corporate and functional responses

The SWOT analysis we outlined in the last section and which is examined in greater detail in Workbook 6, is an important element of the strategic planning process. In that context, it is normal to follow the sequence shown in Figure 2.

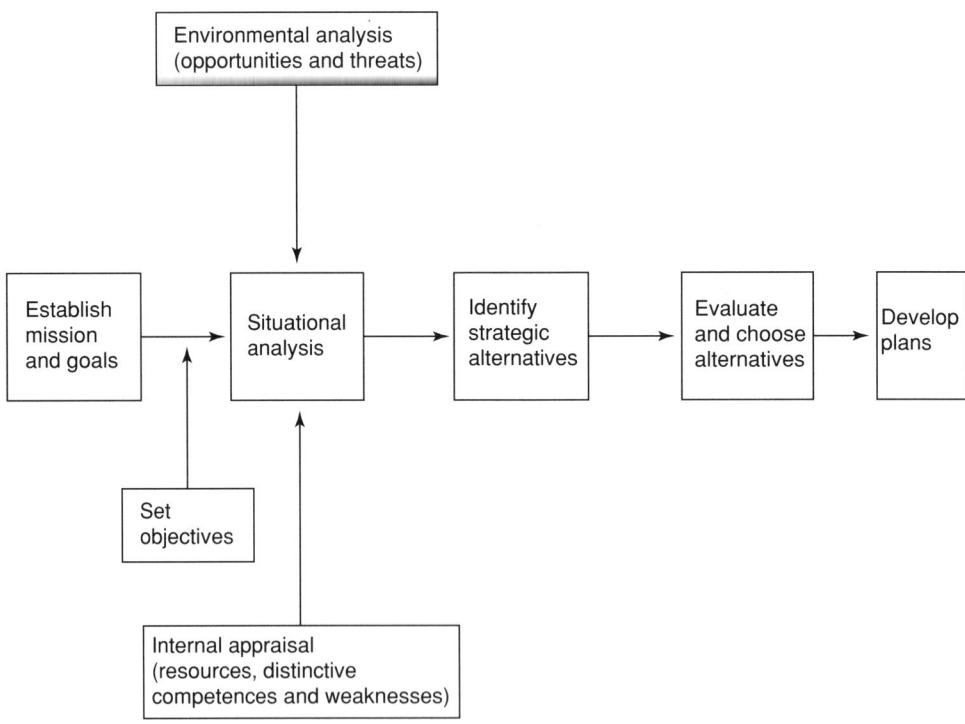

Figure 2 The strategic planning process (adapted from Oliver, 1986)

In this section, we shall explore the range of alternative strategies and the plans to support them that may result from an environmental analysis and internal appraisal.

As the title of this section indicates, all the responses we will examine are either intended for implementation over the long term or else will involve more immediate action, but with longer term benefits.

Some of the actions we shall explore are inextricably linked with the organization's strategy – its mission and goals, the customers and markets it serves. Some of them are corporate, affecting the organization as a whole – its culture, structure, communication policy, for example, fall into this category. Yet others relate to a specific function. As in Section 2, we have used the traditional functional separation into the activities of finance, marketing, operations and personnel.

The approach we have just described is itself based on an analytical, objective and logical view of management and organizations. This is consistent with most, but not all, research into and principles of management practice.

Two examples will give the opposing view. The first is that of Henry Mintzberg, whose research into managerial activity and decision making was presented in *The Nature of Managerial Work* (Harper and Row, 1973). Mintzberg's research showed that, far from spending long and structured periods of time in strategic analysis and decision making, chief executives of both small and large companies spend most of their time in activities lasting fewer than nine minutes, fewer than two hours a day at their desks and were heavily involved in unplanned meetings and talking to people both inside and outside the company. The picture that emerges from this research is one of fragmented short time-scale activity, where decisions are taken 'on the move'.

The second example is taken from a statement by a Rank Xerox manager, quoted by James Brian Quinn (1986).

Typically you start with general concerns, vaguely felt. Next you roll an issue around in your mind till you think you have a conclusion that makes sense for the company. You then go out and sort of post the idea without being too wedded to its details. You then start hearing the arguments pro and con, and some very good refinements of the idea usually emerge. Then you pull the idea in and put some resources together to study it so that it can be put forward as more of a formal presentation. You wait for 'stimuli occurrences' or 'crises' and launch pieces of the idea to help in those situations.

But they lead towards your ultimate aim. You know where you want to get. You'd like to get there in six months. But it may take three years, or you may not get there. And when you do get there, you don't know whether it was originally your own idea – or somebody else had reached the same conclusion before you and just got you on board for it. You never know.

Both examples highlight the contribution of instinct to managerial decisions and the place of vagueness and uncertainty. They provide a useful counterweight to the more usual prescriptions of analytical and evaluative decision making.

ACTIVITY 22

Leaving aside a structured analysis of environmental factors and internal strengths and weaknesses, what does your instinct tell you about the priorities in your organization for long-term improvement?

Strategic priorities and responses

Let us now return to the more analytical approach to problem identification and decision making. Ansoff (1968) defines strategic decisions as follows:

Strategic decisions are primarily concerned with external, rather than internal, problems of the firm and specifically with selection of the product-mix which the firm will produce and the markets to which it will sell ....

Specific questions addressed in the strategic problem are: what are the firm's objectives and goals; should the firm seek to diversify, in what areas, how vigorously; and how should the firm develop and exploit its present product-market position.

Ansoff highlights diversification as a key strategic alternative. However, he does so with major qualifications:

The expansion component of strategy offers strong transfer of product technology or marketing competence, or both. In diversification, novel products are acquired and previously unexplored markets are entered. Therefore, given two otherwise equal opportunities, synergy will be higher in expansion than in diversification. Consequently the firm can expect higher profitability and lower risks from the former.

Put somewhat differently, this means that if a firm can meet all of its objectives by measures short of diversification, it should do so.

Ansoff is here proposing a process which first, compares an organization's forecast performance with its objectives (return on investment, growth rate, product-market performance, for example) and then if there is a gap, evaluates the likelihood of being able to close the gap, based on an analysis of the industries in which it currently operates. It offers the following outline for industry analysis:

1 product-market structure
   a products
   b product missions
   c customers
2 growth and profitability
   a history
   b forecasts
   c relation to industry life-cycle
   d basic determinants of demand
   e averages and norms typical of the industry
3 technology
   a basic technologies
   b history of innovation
   c technological trends – threats and opportunities
   d role of technology in success
4 investment
   a cost of entry and exit – critical mass
   b typical asset patterns in firms
   c rate and type of obsolescence of assets
   d role of capital investment in success
5 marketing
   a means and methods of selling
   b role of service and field support
   c role and means of advertising and sales promotion
   d what makes a product competitive
   e role of marketing in success
6 competition
   a market shares, concentration, dominance
   b characteristics of outstanding firms, of poor firms
   c trends in competitive patterns
7 strategic perspective
   a trends in demand
   b trends in product-market structure
   c trends in technology
   d key ingredients in success

An analysis based on this framework results in two questions, which take us back to the themes of internal appraisal and environmental analysis raised earlier. The questions are:

- does the organization meet the standards of its competitors in this industry?
- if it were to do so, would the industry offer scope for the organization to achieve its objectives?

If the answer to the first question is 'No', but to the second is 'Yes', then the priorities for improvement are functional rather than strategic. However, if the answer to the second question is 'No', then the responses are strategic.

The next activity provides an opportunity to apply this analysis to your own organization.

ACTIVITY 23

What are your organization's objectives?

What is the nature of your industry, using Ansoff's outline for analysis?

❑ Product-market structure

❑ Growth and profitability

❑ Technology

❑ Marketing

❑ Competition

❑ Strategic perspective

Does the industry offer scope for your organization to achieve its objective?

Several models exist to facilitate product-market decisions. All of them, in line with Ansoff, balance the organization's experience and expertise against the nature of the market itself.

Ansoff's own matrix looks like that shown in Figure 3.

MARKET

		Existing	New
P R O D U C T	Existing	Market penetration	Market development
	New	Product development	Diversification

Figure 3 Ansoff's matrix

Ansoff rates these four strategies in order of risk as follows:

Low risk	Market penetration
	Product development
	Market development
High risk	Diversification

The General Electric screen shown in Figure 4 positions (internal) business strengths against industry attractiveness.

Industry attractiveness

		High	Medium	Low
Business strengths	High	✓	✓	?
	Medium	✓	?	✓
	Low	?	✗	✗

Figure 4 General Electric screen

The boxes marked with a tick (✓) are those in which the firm should invest and grow. Those with a question mark (?) are those in which it should move selectively and with caution. Those marked with a cross (✗) are the ones to avoid or get out of.

ACTIVITY 24

What strategic alternatives are open to you in the way of:

market penetration?

product development?

market development?

diversification?

What does the General Electric screen imply for you in the way of:

opportunities to invest and grow?

areas in which to proceed with caution?

those to avoid or get out of?

Corporate priorities and responses

The strategic issues we have just been describing are identifiable through a process of an objective and to a large extent numerical analysis. Equally, the identification of priorities and 'best-fit' responses is also susceptible to quantified assessment. As such, strategic responses follow the model of the rational manager. The softer, more cultural issues we shall explore here are much more dependent on instinct for their identification (although analytical processes can still help and the responses often involve pragmatic and even procedural action).

The issues we shall focus on are organization structure, communication channels and the organization's psychological contract with its staff. All of these themes look forward to the topic of organization culture, which is addressed in detail in Section 6 of this workbook.

ORGANIZATION STRUCTURE

There are many arguments for looking critically at organization structure. The most powerful are those which link structure to the bottom-line performance of the organization. The points they make are that:

- hierarchical organizations are typically ponderous and slow to react
- centralized control reduces motivation and innovation
- multilevel organizations are excessively costly
- decisions taken at the centre are divorced from both customers and staff

Nevertheless, there are opposing views. Goldsmith and Clutterbuck (1985) comment as follows:

In our sample of companies we have, with minor exceptions, two camps. At the one extreme are the decentralists, who operate as federations of independent small units. At the other end are the centralists, who have large functional departments at headquarters and very limited autonomy at operating level. With one exception, the centralists are all retailers; we have so far not been able to find an example of a highly successful British manufacturing company with a heavily centralised organisation. ... The difference between the retailers and other organisations is that the retailers feel there are more areas that need a guiding hand from the centre. The maintenance of margins, for example, is heavily dependent upon central buying.

This central control in multisite retailing is designed to achieve consistency in design, presentation, stock and pricing. Nevertheless, even in this extract, we have a marked preference for decentralized organizations.

ACTIVITY 25

To what extent is your organization structure hierarchical?

To what extent are control and decision making centralized?

Are there good current reasons for this?

How far is it simply the result of history?

Prescriptions for new organization structures are many and various. Tom Peters (1987) suggests:

- a drastic reduction in the number of layers in the organization

  I insist on five layers as the maximum. ... In fact, even the five-layer limit should apply only to very complex organizations such as multi-division forms. Three layers – supervisor (with the job re-defined to deal with a span of control no smaller than one supervisor for twenty-five to seventy-five people), department head and unit boss – should be tops for any single facility.

- the transfer of staff (as opposed to line) positions to functions to operational units

  He argues that 'when you put an accountant (or someone from 'personnel') in the field as a member of a business unit of manageable size, she or he automatically and almost instantaneously changes' and explains this change as becoming more business-minded and outward-focused.

Rosabeth Moss Kanter (1989) confirms these trends, and adds to them a move towards leaner organizations resulting from increased outsourcing and closer supplier relationships. She summarizes her view as follows:

The model for the post-entrepreneurial corporation is a leaner organization, one that has fewer 'extraneous' staff and is thus more focused on doing only those things in which it has competence. In the post-entrepreneurial company, there are fewer and fewer people that are purely 'corporate' in nature; more responsibilities are delegated to the business units, and more services are provided by outside suppliers. And fewer layers of management mean that the hierarchy itself is flatter. Thus, the 'vertical' dimension of the corporation is much less important. At the same time the 'horizontal' dimensions – the process by which all the divisions and departments and business units communicate and co-operate – is the key to getting the benefits of collaboration.

Charles Handy (1989) also emphasizes decentralized structures, but he takes issue with the term and prefers 'federal'.

Federalism implies a variety of individual groups allied together under a common flag with some shared identity. Federalism seeks to make it big by keeping it small, or at least independent, by combining autonomy with co-operation ...

Federalism is not a classy word for decentralisation. ... Decentralisation implies that the centre delegates certain tasks or duties to the outlying bits, while the centre remains in overall control. The centre does the delegating, and initiates and directs. Thus it is that we have that most consistent of organisational findings, the more an organisation decentralises its operations, the greater the flow of information to and from the centre. ...

Federal organisations, therefore, are reverse thrust organisations; the initiatives, the drive and the energy come mostly from the bits, with the centre an influencing force, relatively low in profile.

Handy also develops further Rosabeth Kanter's theme of increased outsourcing, when he describes the 'shamrock' organization:

The organisation of today is made up of three very different groups of people, groups with different expectations, managed differently, paid differently, organised differently ...

The first leaf of the shamrock represents the core workers, what I prefer to call the professional core because it is increasingly made up of qualified professionals, technicians and managers. These are the people who are essential to the organisation. Between them they own the organisational knowledge which distinguishes that organisation from its counterparts ...

Who then does the work? Increasingly, it is contracted out .... All non-essential work, work which could be done by someone else, is therefore contracted-out to people who make a speciality of it and who should, in theory, be able to do it better for less cost ...

The third leaf of the shamrock is the flexible labour force, all those part-time workers and temporary workers who are the fastest growing part of the employment scene. It is cheaper by far, although more trouble, to bring in occasional extra labour part-time to cope with extra hours, or temporary to cope with peak periods.

The next activity summarizes the various suggestions we have reviewed for redefining organizational structures. Use it to identify any approaches that might improve your organization's performance.

ACTIVITY 26

Which of the following might benefit your organization:

Delayering	❑
Transfer of staff responsibilities to operating units	❑
Outsourcing	❑
Federalism	❑
Restructuring the formal organization to a small team of core professionals	❑
Contracting out	❑
Greater use of part-time and temporary staff	❑

COMMUNICATION CHANNELS

There are no communication problems in a one-person business. Marketing knows exactly what operations is doing and why. Operations has a perfect understanding of what is going on in finance. Obviously, because the same individual is responsible for and involved in all of them. But when the owner takes on a partner, or recruits staff, the communication problems start. These problems take many forms:

- inadequate information, resulting in misinformation and rumours
- excessive information, leading to people 'not being able to see the wood for the trees'
- wrong information leading to poor decisions and lack of trust

Effective communication channels should ensure that accurate and relevant information is received by the right people early enough for them to take suitable decisions for themselves and understand decisions by others that affect them.

We can distinguish between four types of communication channels, depending on the nature and purpose of the information they are designed to convey. These are:

- performance reporting systems
- decision information systems
- employee communication channels
- employee involvement systems

Performance reporting systems are intended to transfer control information from operating units to the centre and from the centre to operating units. Increasingly sophisticated monitoring systems and information technology have made this process theoretically very easy to carry out. In practice, the outcome has often been the reverse, as managers at both ends of the communication channel drown in irrelevant and time-consuming statistics. The key questions to ask are:

- what is the minimum information that operating units need about their performance?
- with what frequency?
- what is the simplest way of presenting it so that it leads to effective decisions?
- how little does the centre need to know about unit performance?
- what are the key indicators?
- how can the information needed by the unit and that needed by the centre be derived from the same data?

Decision information systems are intended to allow remedial or innovative action to be identified and taken. Some of this information will be internal and therefore consistent with that needed for performance monitoring – output, productivity, variance from budget, staffing levels and so on.

The rest will be market information – market trends, competitor activity, customer satisfaction levels, for example. Some of this information can be gained formally by identifying key internal indicators and using them to monitor performance, by regular use of market research reports.

The rest – primarily market information – is dependent on the sort of informal techniques regularly promoted by the change manager gurus: listening to the customer, closer supplier involvement, regular external visits, an outward rather than inward focus.

Employee communication channels are intended to ensure that staff know what is going on in the organization. *Employee involvement systems* are there to provide the opportunity for them to influence and contribute to decisions.

Employee communication can be formal – through employee annual reports, employee videos, cascade briefings, notice-boards and so on. They can also be informal – lunch meetings with senior managers, mass gatherings to hear and challenge presentations by senior managers, employee attendance at management meetings, open forums or simply 'management by walking about'.

These information techniques can also be an important source of employee involvement provided that the organizational culture is one in which:

- managers recognize the value of employee participation and do not feel threatened by it
- employees feel committed to the success of the organization
- managers and employees alike have a clear idea of what the organization is seeking to achieve

Now use the next activity to assess the communication channels in your organization.

ACTIVITY 27   A8.3

Is the control information available to operating units relevant, accurate, complete and timely?

Is it easy to understand and make decisions from?

Is control information required by the centre kept to a minimum?

Does it monitor the right things?

Could the needs of the units and the needs of the centre be reconciled more effectively?

How much emphasis does your organization put on:

staying close to the customer?

suppliers as a source of market information?

focus on the external environment?

How does your organization communicate with employees?

How effective is that process?

To what extent does your organization seek employee involvement?

How does it do so?

How far does the organizational process support that process?

THE PSYCHOLOGICAL CONTRACT

In legal terms, a contract involves three elements:

- offer
- acceptance
- consideration

In other words, one party offers to provide a product or service, another party accepts the offer and, at some point, some form of payment or reward changes hands. (That is an over-simplified definition and any business lawyer would throw up his hands in horror at it!)

However, it is worth looking at an employment contract. A job is advertised, interviews conducted, a job offer made. The new recruit starts work. He or she knows what the job involves (from the job advertisement, the interview, the job description, the offer letter) and the reward for it (salary, benefits, working conditions). But what if that were ten, fifteen or twenty years ago? Is the organization now the same as it was that far back? How many of your staff feel that:

■ the organization has moved the goalposts?
■ this isn't the organization I joined?
■ if I'd known this would happen, I wouldn't have come?

The concept of a psychological, as opposed to a legal, contract is fairly straightforward. It starts from the basis that any organization has expectations from its staff, and its staff have expectations from the organization. It then asks:

■ what are these two sets of expectations?
■ are they consistent?
■ if different, how can they be reconciled?

Unfortunately, the speed of change in organizational life has resulted in significant mismatches on both sides. The most obvious and telling examples probably stem from the civil service environment.

The typical new recruit to the civil service twenty years ago was prepared to accept a lower-than-average salary in return for job security, above-average care and support and a relatively undemanding and predictable set of responsibilities. Nowadays, the salary is still typically below-average. By contrast, job security is reduced, care and support are declining and the responsibilities are significantly more demanding and less predictable.

An effective psychological contract should make explicit what the organization expects from its employees, ensure that employees' expectations are consistent with those of the organization and that the reward system provides adequate compensation for the delivery of the organization's expectations. Several factors will affect the nature of this contract:

■ what people are paid for (Length of service? Responsibility? Number of staff? Hours spent at work? Contribution to organizational goals?)
■ loyalty and job security (Should people expect a 'job-for-life'? Is loyalty expected by the organization? Or are staff temporary and expendable?)

- obedience, challenge, innovation (Are staff expected to follow the rules? Or challenge the status quo? Or introduce change?)
- career ownership (Are staff responsible for managing their careers? Or is that down to the organization? Who looks after promotion and transfer? Does the employee ask for training or does the system take care of it?)

Use Activity 28 to assess the psychological contract of your organization.

ACTIVITY 28

What does your organization expect from its staff?

What do your staff expect from the organization?

How much inconsistency is there between these two sets of expectations?

Functional priorities and responses

This final part of Section 5 is not intended to provide an exhaustive analysis of the activities of the finance, marketing, operations and personnel functions. Nevertheless, the sources of, and responses to, a failure to provide an inadequate match between the organizational environment and its internal resources and processes are often to be found in individual functions. The purpose of what follows is therefore to identify the key questions to which individual functions should provide the answers.

FINANCE

- Does the organization have adequate funding to respond effectively to environmental change?
- Does the balance between shareholder and borrowed funding provide adequate decision-making freedom?
- Are turnover, costs and profit appropriately allocated?
- Is revenue expenditure managed and scheduled to meet the needs of the organization?
- Is capital expenditure managed and scheduled to meet the needs of the organization?
- Is the budgeting process effective?
- Are financial controls relevant and suitable?
- Is finance controlled by the centre or the line?
- Is that effective?

MARKETING

- Does the organization know enough about the market that it serves?
- In particular, does it know enough about:
  - customer expectations?
  - competitor activities?
  - trends in demand?
  - potential opportunities?
- Is advertising cost-effective?
- Is promotional activity cost-effective?
- Is the sales force cost-effective?
- Does the pricing structure meet the market?
- Is marketing activity suitably controlled?
- Is there an effective balance between central and business unit marketing activity?

OPERATIONS

- How does product and service quality compare with the industry?
- How does staff productivity compare with the industry?
- Are production resources suited to the current operation?
- Will they be adequate for changes in production requirements?
- Is raw material wastage acceptable?
- Are operational targets and performance adequately monitored?
- Are skill levels adequate?
- Is performance consistent with budget?

PERSONNEL

- How many unfilled vacancies are there in the organization?
- At what levels/in what categories are the vacancies?
- Are reward structures sufficient to attract adequate people?
- Is the recruitment process effective?
- Is the performance appraisal process effective?
- Is the training and development process effective?
- Is the succession planning process effective?
- Do personnel staff have enough contact with the line?
- When people leave, do you know why?

Summary

In this section we have examined the issues around developing a strategy for long-term improvement. Specifically we have covered:

- description of analytic and creative approaches to decision making
- a framework for analysing strategic options
- consideration of the 'softer' issues of organizational structure, communication channels and psychological contracts
- checklists for monitoring performance at individual function level

Section 6
Corporate culture

Definitions

If you have already studied Workbook 6: *Leading from the Front*, you will be familiar with the basic principles of organization culture as they relate to managing change. In this section, we shall be looking at the wider implications of culture and the impact it has on a variety of aspects of organizational performances.

But let us start with some definitions. The trouble is, of course, that organization culture is a 'soft' issue – not susceptible to the sort of numerical analysis with which we started this workbook. As a result, you may find some of these definitions unsatisfyingly vague.

The concept of corporate culture has only been on the management agenda since the 1970s. The first management author to use the term was probably Stanley Davis, whose book *Comparative Management: Organizational and Cultural Perspectives* was published in 1970. We shall return to Davis's ideas on the subject a little later.

However, the fundamental principle of organization culture is a lot older. We can define culture as:

a set of behavioural and attitudinal norms, to which most or all members of an organisation subscribe, either consciously or subconsciously, and which exert a strong influence on the way people resolve problems, make decisions and carry out their everyday tasks. (Clutterbuck and Grainer, 1990)

Or, more simply:

The underpinning values which determine the way we do things round here.

Defined in this way, we can see that corporate culture goes right back to classical management theory. Henri Fayol, one of the fathers of management thinking, published *Administration Industrielle et Générale* in 1916. He based his approach on what became known as the 'functional principle'. This involved:

- a programme of action prepared by means of annual and ten-year forecasts
- an organization chart to guarantee order and assure each person a definite place

- observation of the necessary principles in the execution of command
- meetings of the department heads of every division, conferences of the division heads presided over by the managing director to ensure co-ordination
- universal control, based on clear accounting data rapidly made available.

Fayol further developed this process of forecasting, structure, command, co-ordination and control into fourteen guiding principles: division of work, authority, discipline, unity of command, unity of direction, subordination of individual interest, to the common interest, remuneration, centralization, chain of authority, order, equity, stability of tenure of employees, initiative and morale.

ACTIVITY 29

How would you describe the culture Fayol is advocating?

FEEDBACK

A number of phrases would reflect Fayol's approach:

- a command culture
- centralized decision making
- authorization
- high control

These phrases are equally typical of other early writers on management.

Lyndall Unwick (1891–1983) built on and developed Fayol's headings of forecasting, planning, organization, co-ordination, command and control and promoted a number of principles of good organization, founded on the conviction that a logical structure is better for efficiency and morale than one allowed to develop around personalities.

This *Principle of Specialization* states that, as far as possible, each individual should perform a single function only. The *Principle of Authority* stresses the need for a clear line of authority, known and recognized, from the top to each individual, while the *Principle of Definition* requires that the duties, authority and responsibility for each position, and its relationships with other positions, should be defined in writing and made known to everyone concerned.

Max Weber (1864–1920) identified three different types of organization. A 'charismatic' organization is dependent on a single individual with exceptional gifts or qualities. As the basis of authority is in the characteristics of one person and commands are based on his inspiration, this type of organization has a built-in instability and is bound to face crisis at a time of succession.

A 'traditional' organization bases its operations and ways of working on precedent, custom and usage. Authority and decisions are justified by historical precedent rather than by relevance or rational analysis.

Weber calls his third type of organization 'rational-legal' or 'bureaucratic'. Of course, this latter term has become synonymous with inefficiency, red tape and excessive emphasis on rules and procedures. However, this is not what Weber originally meant. Reverting to his alternative description, the system is rational because processes are designed to achieve specific goals. It is legal because authority is exercised through a system of rules and procedures associated with the position an individual occupies.

Weber's ideal bureaucracy has seven factors:

1 **Specialization**   The work of individuals and departments is broken down into distinct, routine and well-defined tasks.

2 **Formalization**   Formal rules and procedures are followed to standardize and control the actions of the organization's members.

3 **Clear hierarchy**   A multilevel 'pyramid of authority' clearly defines how each level supervises the next.

4 **Promotion by merit**   Staff are selected and promoted on public criteria (qualifications and competence) rather than on the unexplained preferences of supervisors.

5 **Impersonal rewards and sanctions**   Rewards and disciplinary procedures are applied impersonally and in a consistent and formalized way.

6 **Career tenure**   Job-holders are assured of a job so long as they commit themselves to the organization.

7 **Separation of careers and private lives**   People are expected to arrange their private lives so as not to interfere with their work for the organization. Equally, the organization undertakes that the work it expects will be limited to the terms of its contract with the individual.

Although Fayol, Unwick and Weber never refer to 'cultural norms', there are nevertheless several cultural themes running through their work. We can summarize them as:

- specialization
- formally documented tasks and responsibilities
- a clearly defined hierarchical structure
- logic, rationality and predictability
- formalization of procedures
- people as 'cogs in the organizational wheel'

ACTIVITY 30

What organizations do you know which embody this kind of culture?

To what extent does this culture reflect your organization?

What advantages and disadvantages do you see in it?

FEEDBACK

Although this classical or bureaucratic culture is falling out of favour, you will still see it to a greater or lesser extent in:

- government departments (national and local)
- multisite retail businesses, where consistency and control are achieved through rules and procedures
- retail banks, for the same reason
- traditional manufacturing businesses, where specialization is still the norm

We have already mentioned in passing some of the advantages of a bureaucratic culture. For staff it provides security, predictability and a clear idea of individual roles and responsibilities. For the organization itself, it provides a convenient hierarchical structure for exercising command and control.

Nevertheless, it also brings significant disadvantages. Organizations with a bureaucratic culture find it difficult to react speedily to change, because that involves adaptation or replacement of rules and procedures. Security of employment can no longer be guaranteed. It actively discourages innovation and questioning, particularly at lower levels of the organization.

Perhaps the greatest drawback of the culture implied by early management theory is that it suggests there is 'one best way' of managing an organization. Recent writers on culture have taken a very different view. As Charles Handy (1985) explains:

In organisations there are deep-set beliefs about the way work should be organised, the way authority should be exercised, people rewarded, people controlled. What are the degrees of formalisation required? How much planning and how far ahead? What combination of obedience and initiative is looked for in subordinates? Do work hours matter, or dress, or personal eccentricities? What about expense accounts, and secretaries, stock options and incentives? Do committees control, or individuals? Are there rules and procedures or only results? These are all part of the culture of an organization. This culture often takes visible form in its building, its offices, its shops or branches. The kinds of people it employs, their status in society, degree of mobility, level of education, will all be reflections of the culture. The mammoth teaching hospital has a culture manifestly different from a merchant bank, which is different again from an automobile plant. They look and feel different. They will require different kinds of people, will appeal to different kinds. They have different kinds of working. They are different cultures.

ACTIVITY 31

In your view, what factors will influence or determine organizational culture?

Six factors are most commonly quoted:

1 **History and ownership**   Long-established organizations will demonstrate a culture accrued over time and based on what has been successful historically. They will tend to have a more formal culture than newer organizations. Family firms are likely to be more centrally controlled, public companies more bureaucratic.

2 **Size**   Larger organizations tend to be more formalized, specialized and systematically co-ordinated. However, as we shall see later, organizations are currently seeking to avoid the bureaucracy this implies by greater decentralization.

3 **Technology**   Routine tasks are likely to result in a formalized culture. Non-routine activities are better supported in a more relaxed and empowering environment.

4 **Goals and objectives**   An emphasis on productivity and profitability is likely to lead to a bureaucratic culture. Emphasis on innovation will more probably lead to greater delegation.

5 **The environment**   This heading includes the economic, market and competitive environments and the geographical and social environment. As we have already mentioned, a rapidly changing environment demands a culture that encourages flexibility. Differences in national culture will determine aspects of organizational culture such as the importance of the individual, the distribution of decision-making power between the boss and the subordinate, national approaches to uncertainty and the level of emphasis on task achievement on the one hand and interpersonal relationships on the other.

6 **The people**   Many organizations – in particular government departments and the former nationalized industries – have found that cultural change can often be frustrated by the attitudes and expectations of their workforces. Consequently, unless an organization is in the improbable situation of being able to recruit a brand-new workforce, its culture will need to reflect the tolerance for ambiguity, security needs, expectations of personal identity and individual skills and talents of its existing workforce.

Having considered the factors which influence culture, let us now turn to its visible manifestations. Davis (1970) makes a distinction between 'guiding beliefs' and 'daily beliefs':

Guiding beliefs come in two varieties. There are external beliefs about how to compete and how to direct the business, and there are internal beliefs about how to manage, how to direct the organisation. Taken together, they are the roots and principles upon which the company is built, the philosophical foundation of the corporation. As fundamental precepts, guiding beliefs rarely change. They are held in the realm of universal truths and are broad enough to accommodate any variety of circumstance.

Daily beliefs, on the other hand, are a different species. While they are equally part of a corporation's culture, they should not be confused with guiding beliefs. Daily beliefs are rules and feelings about everyday behaviour. They are situational and change to meet circumstances. They tell people the ropes to slip and the ropes to know. They are the survival list for the individual.

Edgar Schein suggests that culture can be recognized from:

- artefacts: physical layout, dress codes, office landscape, slogans
- values: the principles upon which people base their behaviour, often reinforced by stories and myths
- underlying assumptions: these are the source from which the values and behaviours in the organization derive; they may cover the relationship of the organization to its environment, the view of human nature and how people should relate to each other

Now use the next activity to identify the key features of your organization's culture as it relates to boss–subordinate relationships, teamworking, innovation, task achievement, the market and the environment.

ACTIVITY 32

Boss–subordinate relationships

Bosses here are expected to:

- ❏ take firm decisions, command and control?
- ❏ encourage involvement and participation?
- ❏ conform to the rules?
- ❏ treat staff as individuals?

Subordinates here are expected to:

- ❏ follow instructions?
- ❏ contribute to decisions?
- ❏ challenge?
- ❏ act on their own initiative?

Teamworking

Teams here are:

- ❏ permanent, structural units?
- ❏ temporary, task-focused?
- ❏ egalitarian in outlook?
- ❏ hierarchical?

Respect in teams is based on:

- ❑ expertise?
- ❑ status?
- ❑ team role?
- ❑ friendship?

Innovation

New ideas here are:

- ❑ encouraged?
- ❑ carefully evaluated?
- ❑ subject to cost-benefit analysis?
- ❑ unwelcome?

Innovation is seen as:

- ❑ essential to the business?
- ❑ necessary but disruptive?
- ❑ worth rewarding?
- ❑ worth disseminating?

Task achievement

Tasks here are:

- ❑ more important than people?
- ❑ subject to tight deadlines?
- ❑ personal to individuals?
- ❑ expected to meet high standards?

The Market

Customers here are seen as:

- ❑ the main reason for own existence?
- ❑ internal as well as external?
- ❑ deserving of excellent service?
- ❑ the focus for all staff?

Competitors here are seen as:

- ❑ insignificant to most people?
- ❑ sources of good ideas?
- ❑ a major threat?
- ❑ unlikely to affect us much?

The environment

External factors here are:

❑ monitored by everybody?

❑ monitored by specialists?

❑ not seen as important?

❑ seen as offering threats and opportunities?

Environmental changes here:

❑ result in rapid adaptation?

❑ are largely ignored?

❑ provide a stimulus for improvement?

❑ create internal difficulties?

Based on that analysis, how would you characterize the culture of your organization?

Developing and adapting culture

You may be wondering where that examination of culture has got us. The answer to that question is that organizations depend on a suitable culture in order to achieve their goals and objectives successfully.

Davis (1970) argues that, when setting strategy, it is important to measure the degree of 'cultural risk'. One way of doing this is to assess the importance of each element of the strategy, the effectiveness and objectives of the organization, and to measure how compatible each element is with the prevailing culture. Inevitably, a strategy which is highly important to the organization but poorly compatible with the culture will be very difficult to implement successfully and therefore presents an unacceptable degree of cultural risk.

For Schein, the important element in matching culture to strategy is consensus. For organizational culture to support strategy, there needs to be a large measure among managers and staff in five main areas:

■ consensus on the core mission or primary task – What business are we in and why?

- consensus on goals – what specifically is everyone meant to do?
- consensus on the means to deliver the goals – how tasks should be divided up, how performance should be rewarded, how separate activities will be co-ordinated
- consensus on how to measure progress – the reporting and feedback systems to be used
- consensus on remedial or repair strategies – when and how to intervene when things go wrong

ACTIVITY 33   A8.3

In your organization, do any current or proposed strategies present a high degree of cultural risk?

If so, what are they?

To reconcile culture and strategy what will need to change:

❑ the culture?
❑ the strategy?
❑ both?

In your organization, how much consensus is there of:

the core mission?

individual goals?

the means to deliver the goals?

how to measure progress?

remedial or repair strategies?

Activity 33 raised a series of questions which are easy to ask but difficult to answer. In particular, those related to cultural change.

As we have pointed out, organizational culture results from a variety of complex influences, some of which are unchangeable (history, environment) and others which are time-consuming to change (size, technology, people).

The typical response to that problem is through the process of organization development. John Woolhouse (Gower, 1983) describes organization development as:

a planned programme of organizational change designed to help an organization to achieve the strategic purposes and objectives for which it was created.

Organization development is concerned with a wide range of factors:

- structures
- procedures
- systems
- styles of leadership and teamwork
- collaboration between functions and department
- staff motivation
- issues of power and influence
- co-ordination
- the management of conflict

All of these will impact on organization culture.

Woolhouse provides the framework of criteria (Figure 5) against which to assess the extent to which organizational arrangements help or hinder the achievement of its purposes and objectives and to identify priorities for change.

Initiatives required to meet these criteria may include:

- restructuring
- redefinition of tasks and responsibilities
- the introduction of improved communication and/or information systems
- new or revised systems and procedures – or the total abolition of some existing ones
- a new approach to objective setting
- review of reward systems
- the replacement of existing staff
- improved training and development

In view of the scope and complexity of those initiatives, it is important to start a process of organization development by identifying the priorities. Attention and effort must be focused on a limited selection of factors which are critical to successful performance and which the organization has the power to change. Too narrow a programme will be ineffective. Too ambitious a programme will be impossible to implement.

For the next activity refer back to Activity 33 where you identified elements of high cultural risk and lack of consensus.

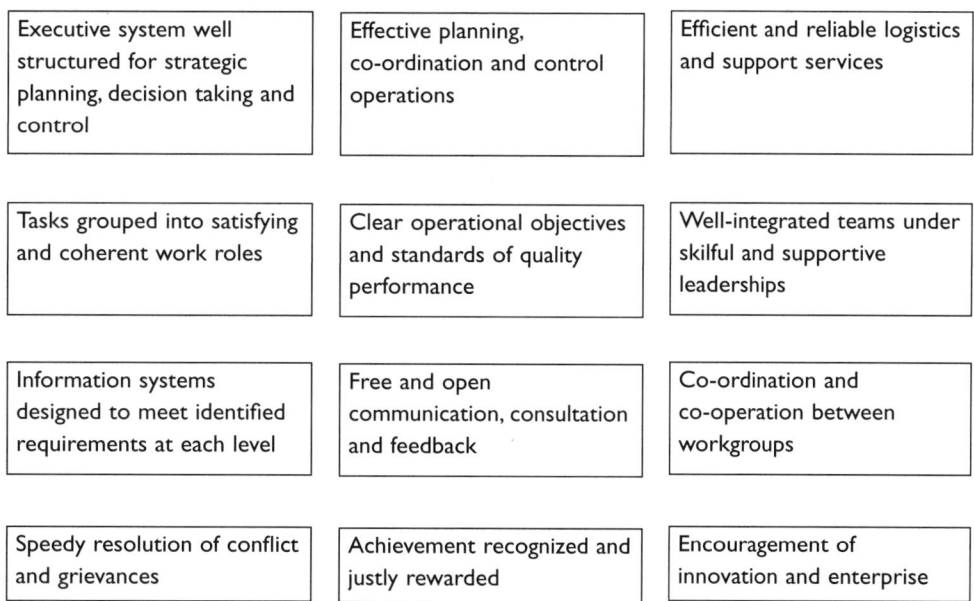

Figure 5   Framework of assessment criteria

ACTIVITY 34

What are the priorities which will need to be addressed to tackle those issues?

	Tick priorities
Executive system for strategic planning	❏
Operational planning, co-ordination and control	❏
Efficient support services	❏
Satisfying work roles	❏
Clear objectives and standards	❏
Integrated teams, professionally led	❏
Information systems	❏
Open communication	❏
Work group co-ordination and co-operation	❏
Speedy resolution of conflict	❏
Achievement recognized and rewarded	❏
Innovation encouraged	❏

Involvement, empowerment and delegation

This heading brings together some of the current buzzwords in organization culture. However, it would be wrong to suggest that they are the only ways forward for a successful organization. As we have pointed out, there is no one 'best' culture – and, in any case, a dramatic shift from a tightly controlled culture to one which suddenly gives everybody a large amount of personal responsibility and autonomy is likely to cause major confusion and, quite possibly, be inconsistent with the abilities and expectations of at least some staff.

Nevertheless, it is important to acknowledge that this is the direction in which organization culture is currently moving. Organizations are stripping-out layers of management ('de-layering') and therefore expecting more from staff who are left. Extensive research has shown that increased responsibility is motivating for many. And workers with high levels of ability and initiative are more likely to be attracted to organizations where they will be able to make use of them.

CASE STUDY

Jacobs, the biscuit manufacturers, are currently going through a painful process of organizational change. Now owned by a French company, they are seeking ways to improve turnover, productivity and profitability, in order to ensure their survival.

Formerly a traditional, hierarchical company, where decisions were taken at the centre and then passed down, they have instigated a major process of internal consultation, at all levels to gain input on the best way forward. For many shop-floor workers, used to senior managers apparently knowing best and giving the orders, this has come as a shock. However, it has also led to an enormous number of suggestions for change and improvement, as well as the identification of several grievances.

It is too early yet to predict the outcome. However, it has proved a valuable source of both concerns and possible solutions, as well as providing some major challenges for senior management.

Workbook 6 of this series stressed the importance of involving people in decisions which would affect them. Any process of organization development can potentially have an impact on a range of stakeholders in the business:

- owners
- suppliers
- customers
- managers and workers

The implementation of change therefore has a much greater chance of success if it involves consultation with those who will be affected by it.

ACTIVITY 35

Who might be affected by cultural change within your organization?

How would you gain input and commitment from them to the change process?

Cultural implications for performance monitoring

An organization's approach to performance monitoring will depend on its culture, because, as we have seen, feedback on performance needs to get back rapidly and efficiently to those who have the authority to take action on it. Consequently, since the level and extent of authority are cultural issues, the shape of an organization's performance monitoring system needs to take account of the places where judgement can be exercised and action taken.

LMG Packaging produces printed paper and plastic packaging for a range of industries, including food and medical supplies. In order to increase production and take advantage of more sophisticated manufacturing technology, the company bought new, computer-controlled machines from Italy. The machines incorporated a range of devices to monitor production tolerances, the outputs from which appear on screens attached to the machines. In order to take advantage of this facility, the company trained its machine-minders to interpret the displays and make adjustments based on them – a task which had previously been done by team-leaders on the old manually controlled machines. They were thus able, not only to enlarge the machine-minders' jobs, but also to restructure the teams, reducing the numbers of team-leaders through transfer and natural wastage.

While, at first sight, this initiative was back-to-front, in that the performance monitoring systems drove the cultural change, it nevertheless provides a practical example of the interrelationship between performance monitoring and culture, as well as demonstrating how technology can impact on culture.

This interrelationship requires answers to a number of questions, not all of them straightforward:

- where, ideally, would you like remedial action on performance to be taken?
- what cultural change, if any, will this demand?
- how will the people affected react to the change?
- do they have the potential and the skills to cope?
- what training will they need?
- what monitoring systems will be necessary?

These questions are both practical and cultural. The answers to them will vary according to a range of considerations:

- whether the performance you are considering is short term, operational or tactical, or long-term strategic
- the level of ability, expertise and sophistication needed to decide on remedial action
- the extent of the cultural change involved
- the attitudes of the people concerned
- the risk and cost involved if things go wrong

ACTIVITY 36

Monitoring short-term performance

At what level is short-term operational performance monitored in your organization?

Could and should that monitoring take place lower down?

Are the people lower down currently capable of taking remedial action?

If not, what would need to happen to make them capable?

Would they react positively or negatively to the change?

If negatively, how could their attitude be improved?

Monitoring long-term performance
At what level is long-term strategic performance monitored in your organization?

How effective is that monitoring?

Might contributions from lower down improve that effectiveness by providing a more operational perspective?

If so, might people lower down also be involved in contributing to remedial action?

Would they and the culture support that change?

If not, how could you promote a more positive response?

Summary

In this section we have examined the importance of corporate culture, and its relationship to monitoring long-term performance and developing the organization. Specifically, we have covered:

- ways of describing and analysing culture
- the importance and influence of culture
- developing and adapting culture
- a framework for organizational development
- the relationship of performance management to organizational change

Section 7 Values, costs and benefits

Values: meanings, uses and limitations

In the previous section of this workbook, we referred to the significance of shared values in shaping an organization's culture, but without specifying what they might be. In this section, we shall first examine in some detail the working relationships and types of decision, both inside and outside the organization, on which an organization's values impact. We shall then present some of the most common schools of ethical thought from which values can be derived and their practical implications. We shall then consider some processes and methodologies for implementing or changing a consistent value system. Finally, we shall review the vexed question of whether values are moral obligations derived from duty to society, or whether they bring tangible benefits to the organization.

Before we start, we need to clear up some of the confusion surrounding the terms used in this debate. We can define an organization as 'a purposive structure designed to achieve a set of pre-determined objectives'. Beyond that simple definition, though, we start to move into areas of significant differences and uncertainties. We have to answer a wide range of questions:

- what should the organization's objectives be?
- for whose benefit should it operate?
- how informal, mechanistic or bureaucratic should the organization be?
- how should its purposive activity be planned, organized and controlled?
- who should be involved in deciding its objectives?
- to whom does the organization owe obligations?
- what is the nature of those obligations?

Try answering these questions now in Activity 37 as they relate to your organization.

ACTIVITY 37

What are its objectives?

For whose benefit does it operate?

How informal, mechanistic or bureaucratic is it?

How (and by whom) is activity planned, organized and controlled?

Who is involved in deciding its objectives?

To whom does it owe obligations?

What is the nature of those obligations?

FEEDBACK

There are almost limitless possible answers to those questions. Much of the variety stems from differences in organizational values.

An organization's values simply reflect its view of itself, its way of looking at the world and the organization's role in it. They determine what is seen as acceptable and unacceptable behaviour, and stem from some fundamental beliefs about what constitutes right and wrong, fair and unfair, just and unjust. Values are purely descriptive. They reflect an organization's ethical standpoint.

That brings us to another terminological confusion. The terms 'ethics' and 'ethical' do not, of themselves, have quality connotations. The subject matter of ethics deals with the fundamental issues of practical decision making, including the nature of ultimate goodness and the standards by which human actions can be judged right or wrong. Only when an individual, organization or society has decided on a set of standards can equality judgements be made, based on whether the individual's, organization's or society's actions are consistent with the ethics it has decided on.

Nevertheless, we tend to muddle our use of the terms. Several writers on business ethics tend to use 'ethical' in the same way it is sometimes used in everyday language. In other words, to define an action or decision as right or wrong, good or bad, according to some absolute standards. The reality, as we shall see later in this section, is that an action that is right according to one set of values or ethical philosophy may be wrong according to another. John Donaldson (1989) quotes the following example of office regulations from a Burnley cotton mill in 1852:

Office Staff Practices

1 Godliness, Cleanliness and Punctuality are the necessities of a good business.
2 This firm has reduced the hours of work, and the Clerical Staff will now only have to be present between the hours of 7 a.m. and 6 p.m. on weekdays.
3 Daily prayers will be held each morning in the Main Office. The Clerical Staff will be present.
4 Clothing must be of a sober nature. The Clerical Staff will not disport themselves in raiment of bright colours, nor will they wear hose, unless in good repair.
5 Overshoes and top-coats may not be worn in the office, but neck scarves and headwear may be worn in inclement weather.

6 A store is provided for the benefit of the Clerical Staff. Coal and Wood must be kept in the locker. It is recommended that each member of the Clerical Staff bring 4 pounds of coal each day during cold weather.

7 No member of the Clerical Staff may leave the room without permission from Mr Rogers. The calls of nature are permitted and Clerical Staff may use the garden below the second gate. This area must be kept in good order.

8 No talking is allowed during business hours.

9 The craving of tobacco, wine or spirits is a human weakness and, as such, forbidden to all the Clerical Staff.

10 Now that the hours of work have been dramatically reduced, the partaking of food is allowed between 11.30 a.m. and noon, but work will not, on any account, cease.

11 Members of the Clerical Staff will provide their own pens. A new sharpener is available, on application to Mr Rogers.

12 Mr Rogers will nominate a Senior Clerk to be responsible for the cleanliness of the Main Office and the Private Office, and all Boys and Juniors will report to him 40 minutes before Prayers, and will remain after closing hours for similar work. Brushes, Brooms, Scrubbers and Soap are provided by the owners.

13 The New Increased Weekly Wages are as hereunder detailed:

Junior Boys (to 11 years)	1/4d
Boys (to 14 years)	2/1d
Juniors	4/8d
Junior Clerks	8/7d
Clerks	10/9d
Senior Clerks (after 15 years with the owners)	21/-d

The owners recognise the generosity of the New Labour Laws but will expect a great rise in output of work to compensate for these near Utopian conditions.

ACTIVITY 38

What is the basic ethical philosophy underpinning these practices?

What values do they reflect?

What other considerations have influenced those values?

How do you react to them?

FEEDBACK

You probably identified the basic ethical position as a Judaeo-Christian one. However, the values they reflect have also been influenced, not only by the social conditions of the time, but also by legal constraints in the shape of the New Labour Laws. (The way in which business ethics are conditioned by geography, society, external influences and historical period is often called ethical relativism. This is a topic we shall return to later, when we explore whether it is possible or desirable to have a consistent set of organizational values across diverse national cultures.) The values probably struck you as conservative, autocratic but also caring, at least to a limited extent. Nevertheless, the owners at the time probably saw them as innovative and forward-looking: another example of ethical relativism.

Organizational values and ethics should provide a coherent framework for individual and organizational decision making. This is easier said than done. The effectiveness of such a framework is limited by the extent to which the values are known, understood and accepted. It is also limited by the extent to which published values and codes of conduct (to which we shall return later) are genuinely endorsed by actual decisions, particularly at a senior level. Predictably, organizational behaviour is influenced much more strongly by the way actions are modelled rather than by the written word, if there is a contrast between the two. The final limit on values comes from the extent to which they support the organization's mission, goals and objectives. The method normally recommended for reconciling the organization's strategic direction with its values, if they contradict, is to undertake the complex process of changing the values. Nevertheless, when values are inconsistent with short-term objectives, experience shows that organizations stand a better chance of success if they accept more suitable objectives and go through an incremental process of amending values and objectives in parallel.

ACTIVITY 39

How well are your organization's values known and understood?

To what extent are they accepted?

Are actual decisions and actions consistent with published values?

Do your organization's values support its strategic direction?

The impact of ethics

In Workbook 6 of this series, we suggested that an organization has a stake-holder relationship with the following groups of people:

- shareholders
- employees
- customers/clients
- suppliers
- lenders
- government
- regulators
- electorate
- public
- pressure groups
- media

The organization's values and ethics will have an impact on all these relationships. They will also affect the balance in the many cases where the organization has to choose between favouring one or other of its stakeholder groups.

Consider the following mini case studies and select the decision you would take.

CASE STUDY 1

The UK clothing industry is characterized by very unequal power relationships between manufacturers and suppliers. UK retailers are extremely large while the typical UK manufacturer is much smaller. If manufacturers do not comply with retailers' terms, the retailer can source their clothes elsewhere.

The UK fashion industry is one of the most price sensitive in Europe, with consumers interested in low-price goods.

Retailers exert pressure on suppliers by retrospective discounts, defect clauses, disproportionate penalties for contract violations and by expecting suppliers to contribute to retailer advertising and mark-downs. These and other tactics have led to low rates of return on capital, low incentives to invest, 'sweat shop' conditions and frequent failure on the part of suppliers. As a clothing retailer, to whom would you give greater emphasis:

customers   ❑
suppliers   ❑

CASE STUDY 2

RJR Nabisco manufactures cigarettes, pipe tobacco, biscuits, cereals, margarine and sweets. Cigarettes and pipe tobacco generate high margins and steady sales in a mature market and consequently generally provide excess cash, which is used to promote the food products, in turn achieving high margins and expanding sales in a growth market.

Expanding corporate profits funded a lifestyle at RJR Nabisco Head Office that was described in the Wall Street Journal as 'a monument of free-spending, nouveau riche excess'. This involved high salaries, generous benefits and perks.

In your view, should RJR Nabisco concentrate on its responsibilities to:

staff   ❑
investors   ❑
the Revenue   ❑

CASE STUDY 3

Most people in the UK only look for a mortgage or pension once or twice in their lives. For most, therefore, the decision relies heavily on the advice of their financial advisor.

In recent years, serious doubts have been expressed about whether that advice genuinely meets the customers' needs, or is influenced by the level of commission available to the advisor. Typically, endowment mortgages carry the highest commission. The problems with mortgage advice have arisen after purchase when mortgage holders have discovered that the mortgage they purchased was deficient in some way – low surrender value of the endowment, for example, or inadequate mortgage protection cover, or insufficient funds to repay the principal in an endowment mortgage at completion.

In your view, who has the ethical responsibility to ensure that customers purchase mortgages suited to their needs?

the customers (caveat emptor)   ❑

the advisors   ❑

the mortgage suppliers   ❑

the regulator   ❑

CASE STUDY 4

Advances in surgery and drugs now make it possible to treat successfully far more illnesses than previously – but the cost is increasing. Hospitals – and consultants in particular – in the National Health Service are regularly faced with painful decisions about the allocation of scarce resources. Traditionally, medical ethics have made it a doctor's responsibility to treat patients as effectively as available expertise allows.

However, the current debate centres round whether decisions should be based on:

- the needs of individual patients, regardless of cost
- the needs of the community as a whole, by making low-cost treatment widely available at the expense of those needing a disproportionate level of expenditure
- the need to keep hospital expenditure within budget
- the allocation of enough money to make suitable treatment available to all, regardless of expense

Where do you stand in this debate? Would you give priority to:

individual patients?   ❑

the community?   ❑

keeping costs within budget?   ❑

making necessary treatment available to all?   ❑

Your responses to all these cases will, of course, depend on the ethical values you bring to the various situations. In each case study, it is possible to justify every one of the positions we have set out. Consequently, there are no absolutely right or wrong answers.

We have deliberately chosen major issues for you to consider. In all of them, your decision will probably have been influenced by economic, legal, social as well as moral or ethical considerations. The same considerations apply to individuals and the day-to-day decisions they take. For example:

- a customer brings back a product to complain that it has failed just after the guarantee expired. Do you replace the product? Dismiss the complaint? Offer a discount on a replacement?
- the job of a loyal employee ceases to be necessary. Do you keep him on anyway? Make him compulsorily redundant? Offer voluntary redundancy? Offer early retirement? Arrange a transfer?
- the work of a small cleaning contractor has deteriorated. Do you find an immediate replacement? Give the contractor warning and time to improve? Re-negotiate the contract price? Work with the contractor to identify the cause and find a mutual solution?

An effective ethical framework or set of cultural values should make it possible for individuals to make decisions concerning all of the organization's stakeholders, with the confidence that these decisions will be consistent with the overall will of the organization and be supported by it.

Values and ethical choices

Moral philosophy has been around for something like 5000 years in the Middle East, 3500 years in India, 2500 years in China and Europe. As you would expect, there is in consequence an almost limitless number of schools of ethical thought. However, many of these represent minor variations on others. It is therefore possible to set out just five major ethical philosophies from which an organization can derive cultural values. They are:

- eternal law
- utilitarianism
- universalism
- distributive justice
- individual freedom

We shall explore each of these in turn.

ETERNAL LAW

Simply put, the philosophy of eternal law states that there is a set of ethical values or principles derived from the mind of God, evident in nature and revealed in religious writing. They are immediately obvious to anyone who studies nature or religious writing, be it the Bible, the Koran or the writings of other religions.

Eternal law sets out a series of rights and duties, the most fundamental of which stem from the idea of divine love – because we are loved by God, we must love others. This reciprocal exchange is summarized in Christian theology by the golden rule: do to others as you would have them do to you.

We looked earlier in this section at a set of Victorian values and procedures derived, at least in part, from the principles of eternal law.

A more up-to-date example is provided in the following case study.

CASE STUDY

Service Master in the USA is engaged in the provision of hospital, school and industrial housekeeping services. It had a net revenue of $2985 million in 1994 and a net profit of $110 million.

Service Master has a set of corporate ethics based on Christian principles. Its goals are:

- To honor God in all we do
- To help people develop
- To pursue excellence
- To grow profitably

Its 1994 Annual Report contains the following statement:

Our philosophy of doing business starts with the belief that people are created in God's image, with dignity and worth; that service cannot be delivered without people, and that quality service cannot be delivered without motivated and trained people.

This foundation of belief challenges us to serve with integrity and adherence to standards of truth and honesty.

Quality and truth are both important. They are, to us, the reality of doing what we say. Our customers expect extraordinary service – performance that surpasses their expectations – and this is our pursuit of excellence.

ACTIVITY 40

What, if anything, do your organization's values have in common with the principles of eternal laws?

What, if anything, attracts you about Service Master's values derived from these principles?

UTILITARIANISM

The emphasis of utilitarian ethics is on the outcomes or results of behaviour. That is, an act or decision is 'right' if it results in benefits for people and 'wrong' if it leads to damage or harm. The objective of utilitarianism is to create the greatest degree of benefit for the largest number of people, while incurring the least amount of damage or harm. The purpose of the philosophy is often summarized as being to achieve 'the greatest good for the greatest number'. The benefits may vary in form, ranging from material benefits to friendship, knowledge, health and all the other satisfactions society considers worth having. The aggregate satisfactions or benefits for everyone in society have to be taken into account.

Not all the outcomes from an act or decision will be positive. Each action will have negative costs and adverse outcomes associated with it. They may include pain, sickness, death, ignorance, isolation and unhappiness. The aggregate harms or costs have to be calculated, then balanced against the benefits to achieve an account of the net consequences.

Utilitarian ethics stress the need to consider long-term, as well as short-term consequences and also the principle that everybody in society should be weighted equally when assessing costs and benefits. One obvious consequent of this is therefore that utilitarian philosophy does not support the analysis we encouraged you to carry out earlier, by deciding which of a variety of stakeholders should take priority when making an ethical decision. The utilitarian view would be that decisions should be taken to achieve the greatest net benefits, both in the short term and in the long term for society as a whole.

In effect, utilitarianism works in a similar way to cost-benefit analysis, although the calculations of net benefit are approximate.

The practical consequences of utilitarian ethics are threefold. They position an organization as a contributing member of society, rather than as a supporter of specific interests. They act as a useful counter-balance to the short termism of which western business culture is often accused. And they provide scope for introducing a degree of mathematical rigour to the process of assessing what is right.

ACTIVITY 41

What, if anything, do your organization's values have in common with utilitarian ethics?

What, if anything, attracts you about the practical consequences of utilitarianism?

UNIVERSALISM

While utilitarianism emphasizes consequences, universalism emphasizes intentions, but it goes further than that. The first fundamental principle of universalist ethics is that we all are required to adhere to a set of absolute moral duties – to tell the truth, to honour contracts, not to take property that belongs to others. The test of absolute moral duties, according to this philosophy, is whether you would be willing to have everyone in the world, faced with similar circumstances, required to act in precisely the same way.

The second principle is that we should treat others as ends rather than means. In other words, everyone is of equal value and therefore no one person's rights should be subordinated to those of anyone else.

The attraction of universalism is that its approach favours absolute standards and so is convenient for the foundation of procedures. For example:

- all bills should be paid within thirty days
- promotion should take account of length of service as well as individual ability
- product prices should be set at a level which makes each product profitable in its own right

ACTIVITY 42

What, if anything, do your organization's values have in common with universal ethics?

What, if anything, attracts you about the principles of universalism?

DISTRIBUTIVE JUSTICE

The philosophy of distributive justice is based on justice as the overriding value of society. It proposes that society is an association of individuals who co-operate to advance the good of all. However, society and the institutions within it are marked by conflict as well as by collaboration.

Collaboration comes about because individuals recognize that joint actions generate more benefits than individual actions. Conflict is inherent because people are concerned about the just distribution of these benefits. Each person prefers a greater to a lesser share and supports a distributive system to ensure that greater share. Such systems can have any one of five different bases: equality, need, effort, contribution, competence.

- education, in theory, is distributed equally
- welfare payments are made on the basis of need
- sales commissions are paid on the basis of effort
- public honours are given to reflect contribution
- managerial salaries reflect competence

Distributive justice asserts that these systems are unjust and leads in the direction of greater equality. Free and rational individuals, recognizing the benefits of co-operation, would accept social and economic inequalities only if they could be shown to result in compensating benefits for everyone, and particularly for the least advantaged members of society. The basic question becomes:

What principles would free and rational individuals, concerned with furthering their own interests, yet wishing to maintain their co-operative efforts, adopt as defining the fundamental terms of their association?

The answer offered by the philosophy of distributive justice is that they would develop a concept of conditional inequality, where differences in benefits had to be justified. They would progress a rule that these differences in benefits could be justified only if they could be shown to result in compensating benefits for everyone, and in particular for the least advantaged members of their society.

In organizational terms, distributive justice has a number of practical consequences. Clearly, by emphasizing greater equality, it runs counter to the excessive 'fat cat' salaries that have received such extensive media coverage. It promotes transparency of reward and benefit systems. It favours structures closer to co-operatives than to hierarchies. And it emphasizes social responsibility, particularly to the disadvantaged.

ACTIVITY 43

What, if anything, do your organization's values have in common with the principles of distributive justice?

What, if anything, do you find attractive about them?

INDIVIDUAL FREEDOM

The philosophies we have described so far emphasize the place of individuals in society. The philosophy of individual freedom recognizes that society is an association of individuals and that co-operation between them is necessary for economic gain. However, it argues that co-operation is the result of the exchange of goods and services. Individuals have the right to make these exchanges voluntarily – they should not be the subject of force – but the basis of ethical decisions should be informed choices about which course of action will lead most effectively to the welfare of the individual.

The philosophy of individual freedom, which has come to prominence since the 1970s, is consistent with the free-market economy of the period and the argument that 'there is no such thing as society'. In practical terms, it reduces the organization's obligations to its staff, emphasizes individual rather than collective bargaining and justifies organizational decisions based on its own welfare rather than wider considerations of other stakeholders, either contractual or other.

ACTIVITY 44

What, if anything, do your organization's values have in common with the principles of individual freedom?

What, if anything, attracts you about them?

Implementing a value system

The obvious starting point for implementing a value system is deciding what those values should be. We have emphasized the need for them to be supportive of the organization's mission and trust that our examination of alternative value systems has prompted some thoughts about the nature of your own organization's values.

The implementation of values has two dimensions:

- values in the bloodstream
- values as a management discipline

'Values in the bloodstream' deals with issues similar to those we considered under the heading of corporate culture. It involves ways of gaining organization-wide commitment to, understanding and acceptance of values as 'the way we do things round here'.

The Institute of Business Ethics publication *Applying Codes of Business Ethics* identifies twelve steps for implementing a code of business ethics. These steps are:

- integration of the code into the running of the business
- endorsement by the chair and CEO
- distribution to all employees

- breaches – what to do when faced with an actual or potential breach
- personal response by employees
- affirmation of the code as a regular procedure
- regular review
- contractual adherence
- training in issues raised by the code
- translation into relevant languages
- distribution to business partners
- Annual Report to include the code

ACTIVITY 45

Which of these steps has your organization carried out?

Which additional steps would lead to the more effective implementation of a value system for your organization?

Bringing values into the bloodstream of the organization is likely to involve:

- incorporating them into the recruitment process as a way of ensuring that all new staff are familiar with and accept them
- consulting and involving staff in the formulation of values, through team briefings, focus groups and union consultation
- modelling values by ensuring that decisions and actions at all levels are consistent with them
- formal processes for monitoring and controlling adherence to the values
- other formal processes, including the publication and distribution of principles, codes of practice, standards and procedures

Several of these, of course, will contribute to the implementation of values as a management discipline. In particular, modelling the values, monitoring and control procedures and their widespread distribution will depend on management commitment.

In addition, the inclusion of values in formal training and disciplinary procedures that not only spell out the consequences of breaching them, but are also rigorously followed, will contribute to this process.

To finish, we shall look at the Institute of Business Ethics recommendation that values should be translated into relevant languages, which raises important questions about the extent to which a multinational organization should implement a consistent value system across a range of different national cultures.

Let us take a broad characterization of the national value systems of three main cultures:

Anglo-American value systems
Hire/fire
Maximization of shareholder value
Emphasis on the bottom-line (concentration on the short term)
Support for free trade
Emphasis on the individual
'Work, job, relax'

Mainland European value systems
Rigid labour regulations/good social benefits
Balance-oriented (profit is necessary for continuity)
Free and managed trade
Emphasis on the social structure of society
'Work to live'

Eastern/Asian value systems
Lifetime employment
Keiretsu: linked relations between individuals/groups
Market-share oriented (long-term goals)
Protectionist
Domination of the groups
'Live to work'

At a simpler level, different cultures take different views of such issues as bribery, time-keeping, the importance of status, the relevance of consultation.

Multinational organizations have tackled this cultural differentiation in one of three different ways, each of which has its own strengths and weaknesses:

- by developing different value systems for different cultures. While accommodating cultural differences, this is clearly at odds with the principle of an overriding corporate culture
- by establishing a detailed value system, to which all subsidiaries are expected to adhere. While giving a clear and consistent message about corporate image, this approach is likely to have a potential negative impact on many stakeholders
- by developing a broad set of high-level corporate values, which different parts of the organization can define and implement in line with the local environment. While accommodating the differences, this approach denies the importance of clear ethical guidelines for corporate decisions

Now answer the questions in the next activity.

ACTIVITY 46

Do organizational values play a role in your recruitment process?

To what extent are staff consulted and involved in the formulation of values?

What action is taken to ensure that decisions and actions model values?

How is adherence to values monitored and controlled?

If yours is a multinational organization, how have you dealt with the issue of differences in national cultures?

How satisfied are you with the effectiveness of your approach?

Ethical values: costs or benefits?

Three factors determine the nature of organizational values:

- external expectations
- the mission and goals of the organization
- internal morality or preferences

At a fundamental level, values that are consistent with all three sets of these demands are likely to bring tangible benefits to the organization.

- its external reputation will be enhanced, increasing demand, support and co-operation
- values which support the mission and goals of the organization are likely to facilitate this achievement
- consistency with internal expectations or preferences should result in higher levels of motivation and staff retention and, other things being equal, greater productivity and less disruption

Consequently, the short answer to the question contained in our heading is that values bring benefits when they are a good match with the environment, the people and the forward direction of the organization. They are costly when there is a mismatch. However, the costs come from the mismatch, not from the values in themselves.

Summary

In this final section we have looked at the ethical dimension of corporate life – how values are and can be integrated into work activities. Specifically we have looked at:

- the importance of values
- schools of ethical thought, and ethical philosophy
- processes and methods for implementing or changing value systems

Summary

The purpose of this workbook has been to provide senior managers with a toolkit with which to:

- identify the key factors upon which the success of their organization depends
- monitor and evaluate its current performance against those key factors
- recognize where improvement in short-term performance is necessary
- elicit support to bring about that improvement
- assess the organization's strategic direction for relevance against its likely future environment and its current resources
- recognize and remedy mismatches
- evaluate the organization's culture and particularly its values for fit with the nature of its operations and the speed of change facing it

The toolkit we have offered has taken several forms. Wherever possible, we have suggested methods and techniques which are susceptible of formal measurement and objective analysis. However, where this has not been possible, we have broken down topics into factor sets which can at least be assessed impressionistically.

At the same time, we have sought to offer the most relevant management thinking on the topics we have covered. In some cases this has been historical, in other current. Some of the writing has come from practising managers, some of it from academics or theorists. As a result, we make no pretence of either simplicity or consistency. Some writers of one generation are violently opposed to the ideas of an earlier generation. Some writers of a single generation are violently opposed to each other!

The overall message of this workbook must therefore be that 'it all depends'.

The systems and indicators you use to monitor performance will depend on the nature of your business, the speed of change and the level of competition.

The ways in which performance is improved will depend on the resources available, the quality of your people and the culture of your organization.

Your future direction will depend on available resources and your future environment.

The need to change the culture will depend on its fits with the business currently and the cultural risk involved in leaving it as it is.

We trust therefore, that this workbook has not appeared to offer any easy solutions! As a result, you may have found it frustrating. If so, we apologize.

Nevertheless, we also hope the workbook has furnished you with enough questions for you to be able to decide the unique combination of approaches necessary for your organization to improve its success.

Recommended reading

Ansoff, H.I., (1968) *Corporate Strategy*, Penguin

Armstrong, M., (1990) *Management Processes and Functions*, IPM

Clifford, D.K. and Cavanagh, R.E. , (1985) *The Winning Performance*, Sidgwick and Jackson

Clutterbuck, D. and Grainer, S., (1990) *Makers of Management*, Macmillan

Davis, S., *(*1970) *Comparative Management: Organizational and Cultural Perspectives*, Prentice Hall

Donaldson, J., (1989) *Key Issues in Business Ethics*, Academic Press

Fayol, H., (1949) *Administration Industrielle et Générale*, Pitman

Goldsmith, W. and Clutterbuck, D., (1985) *The Winning Streak*, Penguin

Handy, C., (1989) *The Age of Unreason*, Business Books

Handy, C., (1985) *Understanding Organisations*, Penguin

Kanter, R.M., (1989) *When Giants Learn to Dance*, Simon and Schuster

Kepner, C.H. and Tregoe, B.B., (1965) *The Rational Manager*, McGraw-Hill

Mintzberg, H., (1973) *The Nature of Managerial Work*, Harper and Row

Naisbitt, J., (1985) *Re-Inventing the Corporation*, Fontana

Nolan, V., (1987) *Problem solving*, Sphere

Oliver, G., (1986) *Marketing Today*, Prentice-Hall

Peters, T., (1987) *Thriving on Chaos*, Excel

Peters, T. and Waterman, R., (1982) *In Search of Excellence*, Harper and Row

Pugh, D., (1986) *Planning and Managing Change*, ed. Bill Major-White, Harper and Row

Quinn, J.B., (1986) *Planning and Managing Change*, ed. Bill Major-White, Harper and Row

Woolhouse, J., (1983) *Gower Handbook of Management*, Gower

About the Institute of Management

The mission of the Institute of Management (IM) is to promote the development, exercise and recognition of professional management.

The IM is the leading professional organization for managers. Its efforts and resources are devoted to ensuring the continuing development and success of its members.

At the forefront of management standards, the IM provides a range of services for its members. These include flexible training programmes and a unique range of support services such as career counselling, enquiry and research facilities and preferential prices on IM publications and other IM products.

Further details about the Institute of Management may be obtained from:

Institute of Management
Management House
Cottingham Road
Corby
Northants
NN17 1TT

Telephone 01536 204222

We need your views

We really need your views in order to make the Institue of Management Open Learning Programme an even better learning tool for you. Please take time out to complete and return this questionnaire to Tessa Gingell, Pergamon Open Learning, Linacre House, Jordan Hill, Oxford OX2 8DP.

Name:..

Address:...

....

Title of workbook:...

If applicable, please state which qualification you are studying for. If not, please describe what study you are undertaking, and with which organization or college:

....

Please grade the following out of 10 (10 being extremely good, 0 being extremely poor):

Content: ....   Suitability for ability level: ....

Readability: ....   Qualification coverage: ....

What did you particularly like about this workbook?

....

Are there any features you disliked about this workbook? Please identify them.

....

Are there any errors we have missed?
If so, please state page number: ....

How are you using the material? For example, as an open learning course, as a reference resource, as a training resource, etc.

....

How did you hear about the Institue of Management Open Learning Programme?:

Word of mouth: Through my tutor/trainer: Mailshot:

Other (please give details):...

Many thanks for your help in returning this form.

Institute of Management Open Learning Programme

This programme comprises seventeen workbooks, each on a core management topic with the latest management thinking, as well as a *User Guide* and a *Mentor Guide*.

Designed for self study through open learning, the workbooks cover all management experience from team building to budgeting, from the skills of self management to manage strategically for organizational success.

TITLE	ISBN	Price
The Influential Manager	0 7506 3662 9	£22.50
Managing Yourself	0 7506 3661 0	£22.50
Getting the Right People to Do the Right Job	0 7506 3660 2	£22.50
Understanding Business Process Management	0 7506 3659 9	£22.50
Customer Focus	0 7506 3663 7	£22.50
Getting TQM to Work	0 7506 3664 5	£22.50
Leading from the Front	0 7506 3665 3	£22.50
Improving Your Organization's Success	0 7506 3666 1	£22.50
Project Management	0 7506 3667 X	£22.50
Budgeting and Financial Control	0 7506 3668 8	£22.50
Effective Financial and Resource Management	0 7506 3669 6	£22.50
Developing Yourself and Your Staff	0 7506 3670 X	£22.50
Building a High Performance Team	0 7506 3671 8	£22.50
The New Model Leader	0 7506 3672 6	£22.50
Making Rational Decisions	0 7506 3673 4	£22.50
Communication	0 7506 3674 2	£22.50
Successful Information Management	0 7506 3675 0	£22.50
User Guide	0 7506 3676 9	£22.50
Mentor Guide	0 7506 3677 7	£22.50
Full set of workbooks plus *Mentor Guide* and *User Guide*	0 7506 3359 X	£370.00

To order: *(Please quote ISBNs when ordering)*

- College Orders: 01865 314333
- Account holders: 01865 314301
- Individual Purchases: 01865 314627

(Please have credit card details ready)

For further information or to request a full series brochure, please contact:

Tessa Gingell on 01865 314477